BAGATELLE

Tony Moss

Keytone

© Tony Moss and Keytone Publications

ISBN 0 9514313 3 1

Keytone Publications
40 Vicarage Road, Sutton Surrey SM1 1QN

FOREWORD

This is the Saga of a family steeped in music.

It has given us much pleasure, some sadness and the means to see and visit much of the World,

To quote Shakespeare:

'If music be the food of love, Play On!!'

Ena Baga

1992

For Ena and Florence . . .
How long the time in friendship grows
With loving memories,
The years of joyous sharing surely knows
The pleasure of knowing
You and You.

Passing phases as in musical phrases
Fill the mind with your sounds, delight.
The high notes the low notes,
Composing or transposing
Make moments so full of light.
Let time remember
You and You
Ena and Florence.
22nd July 1992 A.F.G.J.

BAGATELLE

CHAPTER ONE

This is the story of a Queen, not we think of Royal blood, but a 'Queen of the Keyboard'. It is also about her talented musical family and the countless friends and colleagues, some of them famous, with whom she has been associated during seventy years in the world of entertainment.

Born on 15th January 1906 at 45 Colebrook Row, off the City Road and near the Angel Islington, she was christened Ena after the Queen of Spain. The Royal Ena, daughter of Princess Beatrice and Henry of Battenburg, and grand-daughter of Queen Victoria, was in the news in 1906 as she was to marry Alfonso XIII, King of Spain on May 21st of that year. Returning to the Royal Palace after the ceremony, a bomb was thrown at the new Queen Ena's coach and she and the King were lucky to escape with their lives.

The two Ena's never met but Ena Baga was much later commanded to appear at Balmoral before King George V and Queen Mary, who, as the Prince and Princess of Wales, had been present in Madrid on that near fateful day. But, we are jumping ahead. Ena, the future 'Queen of the Keyboard', was the fourth daughter of Constantine Joseph Baga, born in Liverpool, the son of an Italian and whose mother came from Cork. There was also Italian blood on her mother's side, again one generation away, and her mother's maiden name was Draghi. Her mother's father had a flair for stocks and shares and had been pretty successful, whereas her father's father was a devotee of Donizetti and Italian composers of opera and sang opera in Italian all day long! He had come to England with Giuseppe Garibaldi, who he recalled had kissed the ground when they disembarked at Folkestone.

Eyre Street Hill, leading down to Clerkenwell Road, was very much the Italian Quarter in the Nineteenth Century, with an Italian Church and Italian-run Ice Cream and Coffee Shops, and Ena's father, being fluent in both languages, used to attend the Italian Court at Clerkenwell to interpret for the immigrants. Ena also had an uncle who was responsible for all the electrical gear at the nearby Royal Agricultural Hall, known as the 'Aggie', and which from the opening in 1862 had staged everything from cattle and horse shows to circuses, wrestling, walking and cycling races and even bullfights! The 'Aggie' was also the home of the World's Fair, and at one of these little Ena, no more than three or four, was confronted (hand-in-hand with Aunty 'Mick') by an enormous engine that terrified her. She remembers rushing past it, hotly pursued by the anxious Aunty Mick.

Constantine Baga was a musician of some ability. Not only did he conduct orchestras but he was also an accomplished harpist and pianist. The Cinematograph Act of 1909, enacted on 1st January 1910, provided for the licensing of all premises where films were shown to the public and for stringent safety regulations, including a separate enclosure for the projection equipment. The nitrate film used was highly inflammable and had caused some nasty fires. You might think that this legislation would put a curb on the growth of the cinema, but just the opposite happened. The Act had the effect of giving a measure of respectability to this new

The four Baga belles – Beatrice, Ena, Celeste and Florence.

art form and would be entrepreneurs realised that, far from being a five-minute wonder, films had come to stay. Purpose-built cinemas mushroomed all over the UK; whereas Islington, where some of the earliest cinematograph shows were given in 1896 at Collins' Music Hall and at the Agricultural Hall, saw the rise of the Empress Electric in Upper Street in 1910 and the Coronet in Essex Road in 1911.

In November 1912 yet another picture house opened in Islington, the Victoria in New North Road. Chris Draper ('Islington's Cinemas & Film Studios') says that 'Cloggy', the Victoria's pianist, was a bit of a comedian; 'sometimes he'd play a sweet melody during a fight scene, and, when the hero and heroine finally embraced, he'd belt out a stirring march.' Chris says that the audience would show their appreciation with a shower of orange peel and peanut shells! Someone must have been over-zealous one evening, as 'cloggy' landed in hospital! The owners asked Ena's father if he would take over at the Victoria but 'Con' Baga said he would only do so if they covered the orchestra pit with wire-netting. This proved to be quite unnecessary as he was a sympathetic accompanist to silent films and the audience loved him.

In March of the following year, 1913, a splendid cinema opened in Islington High Street, just a few doors from the Angel Hotel. Aptly named the Angel Picture Theatre and surmounted by a tower capped with a pavilion with oeil-de-boeuf windows, it was – for its time – luxurious, with chandeliers, stained-glass windows and striking plasterwork in a 1,400-seat auditorium. Constantine Baga was lured away from the Victoria to conduct the Angel orchestra, augmented by a small

2

2-manual church-type ('straight') pipe organ by Norman & Beard of Norwich (they amalgamated with Wm Hill & Son three years later).

Ena's father was an expert in the orchestral accompaniment to films and he was the first to 'fit' music to the mood of the movie rather than just playing anything, which was the general rule. His competitors heard of this and would come and lean over the orchestra rail to see what he was using! However, Constantine got wise to this and stuck brown adhesive paper over the music titles. As we shall see, the family began to follow in father's footsteps.

Con Baga's first child (and they were all girls!) was born about 1892 and given the lovely names of Celeste Madelaine. She had a tremendous sense of humour and fun, and she was Ena's favourite of all the three sisters. Celeste was kind, considerate and gentle, with brown eyes and very straight hair. Once asked what she had been doing when she had been closeted in the bathroom for a lengthy time, she replied 'my hair is as straight as sticks!'. She was not bossy like her younger sister Florence, nor did she have the drive that Florence had. Ena says that she did not sufficiently assert herself during her life, and her future husband, Hans, caused her a lot of heart-ache. She spoke fluent Italian.

Celeste was at first trained to be a concert pianist and showed great talent. Ena says that she had a phenomenal natural technique, and she was a brilliant sight-reader. Theatre and cinema were in the family's blood, and when 'The Waltz Dream' opened with Lily Elsie at Daly's Theatre in Leicester Square in January 1911, the Ladies' Orchestra featured on stage had as its pianist – Celeste Baga! 'The

Constantine (Papa) Baga – in serious mood.

Mama Baga at Southend, with suitable nautical background!

3

Celeste Baga – divinely good.

Beatrice Baga in 1933. Ready for 'The Gipsy Princess'?

Waltz Dream' ran for four months at Daly's, whence Celeste moved to the Pavilion Cinema, Marble Arch, laying piano to silents with the pit orchestra under M.D. William Trytle.

The second daughter born to Charlotte and Constantine Baga was Beatrice Charlotte – two years after Celeste. Beatrice also had a royal name, after Princess Beatrice, Queen Victoria's ninth child and mother of the future Queen Ena of Spain. Unlike sister Celeste, Beatrice had tight, curly black hair, but she did have the family's sense of humour. She was always joking, and was frequently the life and soul of any party. When she got excited, and in her eagerness to get a story across, she would develop a stutter. She was fond of kindling harmless mischief and was a real 'firebrand' of a lady. In later life, she much envied Florence and her life-style.

Beatrice learned to play the violin at a very early age and took up the saxophone, displaying the family's musical talent. She looked extremely good on stage, especially in her gypsy costume. Beatrice joined her sister Celeste at the Marble Arch Pavilion in 1911, and they both deputised for other instrumentalists throughout the West End of London, including the Stoll Theatre Kingsway. After 1913, they both joined their father at the Angel Islington, as a pianist and violinist in the cinema orchestra. It was not long before they were joined by a fourth member of the family.

The third baby girl was born on 1st August 1896, by which time the family had moved to Oakley Crescent, a little further along the City Road. Grandfather Baga suggested she should be named after 'la bella cita' – the beautiful city of Florence. Florence Baga possessed all the characteristics of those born under the sign of Leo. She had a dynamic personality and liked to impose her will on others; she quickly became angry – but equally speedily forgot and forgave; she was outspoken but of a good disposition; she craved the limelight, was ambitious, and achieved the highest honours through her dynamic personality. Florence liked luxury and pleasure, and tended to dress extravagantly – sometimes appearing a little overdressed. Generous to a fault, she became an accomplished member of her profession, loved by countless friends and admirers.

Mama Baga considered Florence to be the one she could trust, especially in money matters. Papa Baga was passionate but not so practical (he would sometimes bring people to their home unexpectedly, much to Mama's consternation), so Florence was the one Mama would discuss matters with, as she seemed to have a practical turn of mind. Because she was level-headed and (perhaps encouraged by Mama's confidences) developed a marked bossiness, all the other girls in the family would frequently row with Florence. This rather strengthened her will and inherent obstinacy, which was very evident in later life.

At the age of about seven or eight, Florence got in the way of one of her father's rifle shots, catching a bullet in the forehead. No serious damage resulted, but for the rest of her life Florence bore a white streak in her hair – something her hairdresser told her people paid large sums of money for! In 1910, at the age of only 14, little Florrie obtained the job of pianist at Terry's Theatre in the Strand, also playing for films at the Victoria Picture Hall next-door, where all seats were sixpence! 'It was rather a doubtful film for the times', she remembered. 'At the end of the week's run I got my pay of 25s., which was good money then. The manager asked me for my name and address for the cinema's records. When I told him I was only 14½ he was astounded and said I could not play anymore in his theatre.' It was the only time she got the sack! In 1914 Florence joined her father and sisters at the Angel Islington, and Mr. Williams, the organist, taught her to play the Norman & Beard organ. So, Father Baga and three of his daughters were all together under the wings of the Angel, so to speak, when the fourth daughter, Ena, was beginning school and taking music lessons. History was in the making!

'Music in the family at Southend . . .'

CHAPTER TWO

From five years of age, Ena attended school at St. John's Convent, at the northern end of Duncan Terrace, close to Upper Street. She was made to don her best dress for church on Sundays, and new, squeaky shoes. When the Baga family made their entrance to St. John's Church, all eyes turned to look on account of Ena's squeaky shoes. (*My* father's used to squeak when he went forward with the collection, and I was always embarrassed because I felt it disturbed the reverence and tranquillity of the offering). Next to St. John's Church at the Convent, Sister Sylvester tried to teach Ena the piano, but Ena didn't like her and ran to hide under the table! In view of the nun's name, dancing might have been more appropriate! Ena's father suggested that she should learn typing and shorthand, but this was not to her taste and she asked if she could continue music with another teacher. She was then sent to Eden Grove College, Holloway, to the strict order of Notre Dame de Sion, where Mass was held every morning.

In the meantime, the family had moved to No. 7 Canonbury Square. One night, not long after the war had started, Constantine called the entire family to the porch to see a Zeppelin overhead (it later came down at Cuffley, near Potters Bar). Mama pointed out in no uncertain terms that Papa was standing on the top step of their porch wearing a short shirt but no trousers!

Like all with an artistic temperament, Ena was a sensitive child and the strict order of Notre Dame de Sion had a bad effect upon her. This, together with a weakness of the chest, made her ill. By the time she was ten years of age (1916), the family doctor was strongly advising sea air. Mama, Papa and Ena therefore packed their bags and went to live at Southend-on-Sea, at No. 132 Southchurch Avenue. Ena was much happier and, having continued with her music lessons, was appointed organist at the Church of the Sacred Heart, Southchurch Road, in 1918, at only 12 years of age! Her father was the Choirmaster and he introduced Gounod Masses and Gregorian plain chant masses. Ena also attended the Roman Catholic School of the Sacred Heart.

Sisters Celeste and Beatrice were now in their mid-to-late twenties and both had married. In fact, they married Danish brothers, Hans and Christian Palle respectively, but carried on with their careers. Before she met Hans, Celeste had played at various cinemas, including a spell as pianist with Van Dam and his orchestra at the Regent Street Polytechnic Cinema, where, incidentally, the first public film shows in the UK were given by the Lumiere Brothers of Paris in February 1896. At one of the cinemas, the manager was a Mr. Lou Morris, who, much against his parents' wishes, went into the cinema business. He was very attracted to Celeste and asked her to marry him, but Father Constantine wished his daughters to marry Roman Catholics and refused permission. However, that is not the last we shall hear of Mr. Lou Morris!

When the younger and beautiful Florence started courting, Ena had to play the part of chaperone, which must have been quite daunting for a girl nine years her

Beatrice leading the orchestra at the Kursaal Ballroom, Southend.

sister's junior. Florence's suitor, a Mr. Marshall, gave Ena a box of chocolates every time they went out, but when Florence transferred her affections to Bandleader Harry de Jong, Ena got only a bar of chocolate! By 1918, Florence had made great progress as an organist and had transferred from the Islington Angel to the Rink at Finsbury Park, which had opened on the site of a tramway depot as the Finsbury Park Cinemamatograph Theatre (Pyke's circuit) in 1909. The organ was a straight one by Jones of London, replaced in 1926 by a Wurlitzer.

While visiting the family at Southend in 1918, Florence and Harry, now married, met a certain Mr. Percy, who was a friend of Quentin Maclean, then Assistant Organist at Westminster Cathedral and about to take up his first cinema post at the Grand Fulham, followed by the Globe Acton. Mr. Percy was installing a 4-manual Hill, Norman & Beard straight organ in the Strand Cinema, Warrior Square, Southend, which had opened in 1911, the conversion of a skating rink. Harry de Jong was conducting the orchestra at the West End Cinema Theatre (later Rialto) in Coventry Street, above the Café de Paris, and described as the finest of the pre-first world war central London picture houses. At the opening in 1913 it made a great impression with the first Neon sign in London's West End. Percy asked Harry to go to Southend to become Musical Director at the Strand. There was a Grand Opening of the newly-renamed Strand in 1920, with a church organist, whose opening recital fell so flat that, in desperation, Percy telephoned Florence at home in Southend to save the day. Florence always maintained that she intended to forsake music for the role of a housewife when she set up home at Southend, but, fortunately for us, after initial reluctance she went to the theatre and brought the house down with a selection from 'Chu-Chin-Chow'. She got the job!

Quentin Maclean got to know Florence and Ena well, and, as he had a great liking for the Hill, Norman & Beard organ, he would come down to Southend on his day off from the Globe Acton, or the Regent Brighton (where he played a similar instrument from 1921 to 1924) especially to play at the Strand. In 1924 'Mac' went to the Pavilion Shepherd's Bush to become resident at the second 'unit' organ to be installed in a UK theatre (the first was at the Surrey County Cinema, Sutton in 1921 – both by Compton), and in 1928 he opened the giant Christie theatre organ, in the design of which he had played a large part, at the Regal Marble Arch. From 1930 to 1939, 'Mac' presided at Europe's largest Wurlitzer, the 21-rank instrument at the Trocadero Elephant & Castle, where, in the words of his signature tune, he 'knocked 'em in the Old Kent Road'. A genius in the interpretation of both light classics and pop tunes of the day, he will always be remembered for his recitals and broadcasts, and of course his many recordings.

Beatrice's husband, Christian, was a double-bass player, and when Harry and Florence had settled in at the Strand, Beatrice and Christian were asked to join the de Jong Orchestra as violinist and double-bass player respectively. They moved into the flat above Harry and Florence at No. 128 Southchurch Avenue, while Celeste and husband Hans also came to Southend to live, in a flat above Ena and the parents at No.132. The whole family were together again and living within a few doors of each other!

At this time something strange and very sad occured. Celeste and Hans had a small daughter named Violet, who fell down at the local Catholic School and cut her knee badly. Prescribed ointment proved inadequate, and meninigitis set in leading to the child's death. Beatrice and Christian had a son, Harold, who was asleep on the night that Violet lay dying at No. 132. In his sleep, Harold heard from No.128 the child crying and, sleep-walking, made his way along the few yards to the house of the sick child. Grandfather Constantine wrote to Conan Doyle, describing the undeniably psychic call to the cousin from the dying Violet, upstairs at No.132, two doors away. Sadly, Celeste and Hans had no further children, and later Celeste divorced Hans on grounds of adultery. She married a Dutchman Alec Coenen, also a musician.

At school, Ena gained a very close friend, Norah Green, later Mingay. Although Ena moved away from Southend in 1926, they kept in touch and Norah was the first guest on Ena's 'This Is My Life', presented by me at Gunton Hall, Lowestoft, more than sixty years later. Father, Constantine, secured a post at the Technical College, teaching French and Italian (in both of which he was fluent), but eventually set up his own business, an antique shop near Southchurch Road. Ena left school at age 14, in 1920, and her first job was playing for 'Thé Dansant' at Southend's Palace Hotel. She got so bored she used to prop a book up on the piano, usually Edgar Allan Poe, but a message came down one afternoon to the effect 'Miss Baga, we do not pay you to sit and read books in public'. If she played at the Palace on her own without another member of the family present, her father always met her afterwards. 'Don't talk to any strange men', he would say. One night, during severe winter weather, a very nice man offered to help her home, but, remembering father's advice, she refused, saying she was quite capable. In her own words, Ena promptly 'took a pearler' down the hotel steps into the snow! The 'kind man' put her into a taxi.

Next, Ena took her first job in a theatre, at the Palace Westcliff, a lovely little theatre opened in 1912 with a colour scheme of Rose du Barry and gold. The Palace had 'bioscope' shows right from the beginning and it was for a mixture of live and film shows that Ena played piano in the Pit, doubling on violin for musical productions and even reaching Second Violin (Philip La Riviera taught Ena the violin). When playing solo, she would stare at the Conductor, who couldn't help laughing! If Papa was in the audience, he would say 'Are you listening, Harry?' The Palace is still a pretty theatre, in red and gold.

Between 1920 and 1925, Ena also played piano for silent films at various Southend cinemas, including Garon's in the High Street, which had a café next-door also owned by the Garon family; the Mascot Westcliff in Leigh Road; and the Rivoli in Alexandra Street, a reconstruction to the plans of George Coles of the Empire Theatre of 1896, re-opening as a cinema in 1921. Sisters Celeste and Beatrice were also playing in Southend cinemas at that time, Celeste becoming resident at the Rivoli for some years.

The reader may wonder why all four sisters took up silent film accompaniment, when, with such inborn talent, one would think they would look towards solo performances. As children, they all went to the Angel Picture Theatre as a treat to watch Papa, and the art of silent film accompaniment was therefore instilled into

PALACE HOTEL, SOUTHEND-ON-SEA.

Where it all began for Ena – thé dansant at the Palace Hotel, Southend-on-Sea. To the left of the hotel was the Ritz cinema, which organ Ena played at Blackpool Odeon in 1948.

them at an early age. Just as they were all growing up during the first decade or two of the 20th Century, cinemas mushroomed and there was a tremendous demand for accomplished musicians, particularly pianists, as many of the smaller halls could only afford a pianist, sometimes augmented by a violinist; not to mention the orchestras of the more opulent houses from around the first-world war onwards, until the advent of 'talkies' in 1928. As a child, Celeste was taken by her father to one of the musical academies, but she had such an amazing natural technique that the tutor said there was nothing he could teach her! This inherent technique that they all possessed, in varying degrees, plus the excitement instilled in them as they watched their father at the Angel, inevitably led them to the same profession.

The essential qualities for expert film accompaniment are a good memory, an absolute library of music in the brain (e.g. if the film is set in Germany, think of German composers) and experience. Experience teaches you to develop a sense of what is coming next. In other words, you learn to anticipate. Playing with a cinema orchestra, one would have three cards with different themes for 'lovers', 'the villain' and a 'battle scene'. The conductor would give a coded tap for each theme to the orchestra and the orchestral organist. The organ was not always required for the main feature but the orchestral organist would be expected to cover the second feature. When Florence and Ena were together at the New Gallery in the twenties, they played for films like 'Intolerance' which, four hours long, would have an intermission, Florence and Ena playing for half each. In the early days of 'talkies', a Sound Manager would sit at the back of the stalls and signal the projection-box to increase or decrease the volume. The orchestras were for the most part dismissed, but organists were retained to play in the interval and to cover for break-downs which were not infrequent.

The film 'Coquette' featured a well-known star with a terrible voice. She had been popular as a star of the silent screen but the manager said to Florence 'For God's sake, play some quiet sentimental music as a background to ease the pain of that voice!'.

One might also wonder why a pipe organ, an instrument with such a strong association with the church, should also become part of the cinema? As I have said, the smaller cinemas could not afford orchestras and often had to make do with a piano, sometimes augmented with violin and occasionally percussions. Neither was really satisfactory, as a piano has limited range in tone and volume, and, apart from the fact that they were expensive, the orchestras could not always have a run-through before a film performance and only the very best of them could fit music to the mood of a film. The organ is much more versatile, and the organist is able to change the mood at the drop of a hat, often improvising for short passages.

The first pipe organ we know of in a cinema in the UK was installed at the Palace Tamworth in 1909. The cinema possessed a Harper Electric Piano for the accompaniment of its pictures, and in 1909 John Compton of Leicester added six ranks of pipes and percussions. Church-type ('straight') organs were installed from 1910 onwards, e.g. by Jones of London at the Palladium Brighton, Pavilion Brixton, Blue Hall Edgware Road, Rink Finsbury Park, Marlborough Holloway; by Nicholson & Lord at the Grange Kilburn and Stoll Picture Theatre Kingsway; and by Brindley & Foster at the Heeley Electric Palace Sheffield, where

The young Ena, on holiday at Herne Bay with Cousin Albert.

Florence with her first husband, Harry de Jong.

the M.D. from 1923 to 1928 was the soon to become famous Reginald Dixon!

It was realised that these basically church organs were not suitable and in 1910, an Englishman by the name of Robert Hope-Jones pooled his revolutionary ideas for the organ with the Rudolph Wurlitzer Co in the USA and the unified theatre organ, or 'Wurlitzer Hope-Jones Unit Orchestra' was born. John Compton installed the first unit organ in the UK at the Surrey County Cinema, Sutton, in 1921, but it was not until 1925 that the first three Wurlitzers were opened in England, and they were at the Picture House Walsall, Palace Tottenham and the New Gallery, Regent Street, London. The latter cinema will play a big part in our story, but for the moment back two years to 1923 and to Southend-on-Sea.

Ena made her debut as a concert artist one wet Sunday evening on Southend Pier, with rain pouring through the roof! She played 'Autumn' by Chaminade, for which she received the princely sum of ten shillings and a glass of port. Being just 17, the port went to her head and she couldn't find the last bars of 'Autumn'. When she eventually finished, she was told in a best stage-whisper to take a bow, and, seeing everything through a haze, she bowed to the back of the stage, presenting the audience with her back-side rather than her best side!

It seemed that the Baga family were all happily settled by the sea at Southend, with all four sisters and the three husbands engaged in their musical professions. But the scene was soon to change.

At no. 121 Regent Street, London, a private art gallery had existed since 1888. In 1910 it was converted into the New Gallery Restaurant & Wiener Café, but this was

12

Florence Baga – Italianate beauty.

remodelled as the New Gallery Cinema and opened as such on 14th January 1913. In 1920, Provincial Cinematograph Theatres, who had been looking around the West End for a London showcase, bought the New Gallery and the Les Gobelins Restaurant alongside. In 1924 the cinema was rebuilt and enlarged to seat 1,450, and re-opened in June 1925 with a Wurlitzer (only the third one to be opened) and orchestra. The Manager of the Rink Finsbury Park, by then controlled by PCT, was one Bill Evans and he remembered a young lady organist who, back in 1918, had shown great promise. Evans contacted the de Jongs, offering Harry the leadership of the orchestra, a grander affair than that of the Strand Southend, and Florence the post of organist. Florence always said that she was asked to be the solo organist but she protested that she would not wish to have to wait around until the final curtain, i.e. when Harry and the Orchestra would be free, and plumped for the job of Orchestral Organist, playing with the orchestra. So it was, and the solo appointment was given to Jack Courtnay of the Stoll Picture Theatre, Kingsway. Jack Courtnay, real name Taylor, was born in Scotland in 1895 and began his career just after the First World War touring in Canada and the USA. He came to England in 1923 to the King's Sunderland, followed by the Stoll, and had opened the first two British Wurlitzers for PCT at the Picture House Walsall and the Palace Tottenham. He remained at the New Gallery for only one year, opening further Wurlitzers for PCT at Glasgow and Leicester, before going to the Plaza Piccadilly for Paramount. He returned to the USA in 1928, returning again to the UK in the 30s to open organs at Poole, Neath, Tooting, Hoddesdon, Limerick, etc. He spent two years at the Regal Marble Arch, followed by County Cinemas, and then formed his own band. For most of the Second World War he worked in the Borough Engineer's Department at Southend, and his last theatre organ appointment was at the Empire Leicester Square from 1945 to 1948. Although he opened many theatre organs, his residencies rarely lasted more than two years. Curious!

The vacancy at the Strand Southend was filled by – yes, you've guessed it! Ena Baga! Unfortunately, after only one year the Strand was completely destroyed by fire, apart from the projection box and paydesk. The only remains of the organ were the two balanced swell-pedals. I mischievously suggested to Ena that it might have been one of her cigarettes, but she vehemently protested that she did not smoke in those days! She doesn't now.

Knowing that Ena had lost her job, Bill Evans of PCT asked her to come and join her sister Florence at the Kew Gallery, which she did in 1926.

CHAPTER THREE

As I have said, the Wurlitzer at the New Gallery Regent Street was the third one to be opened in the United Kingdom, and it was the first to make a real impact. The previous two Wurlitzers, at Walsall and the Palace Tottenham, were small organs of six ranks of pipes only (Model 'D') and the New Gallery organ was the first Model 'F', a sweet instrument of eight ranks of pipes, installed to the right of the stage, with the console on the same side, i.e. to the right of the orchestra, close to exit doors which Ena says made it a very draughty spot! When Jack Courtnay left in February 1926, a comparatively unknown Reginald Foort took his place, having made his first acquaintance with the Wurlitzer organ only the previous year when he opened the fifth UK Wurlitzer at the New Picture House, Princes Street, Edinburgh. (The Princes St. Wurlitzer was removed in 1938, enlarged to 10 ranks and installed in the Granada Kingston-on-Thames in the dark days of 1939, where it was re-opened by Reginald Dixon of Tower Blackpool fame).

Reginald Foort, born at Daventry in 1893, had the usual groundwork as a church organist, becoming Assistant at Holy Trinity Paddington in 1909 (at the age of sixteen) and Organist at St. Mary's, Bryanston Square. His first cinema appointment was as Assistant to Leslie James at the Marlborough Theatre Holloway in 1919, a superb theatre by the celebrated architect Frank Matcham that had become a full-time cinema the year before. From there he took the giant step of opening his first Wurlitzer at Edinburgh in 1925 and must have made a great impression on the PCT management, as he was posted to the West End Flagship, the New Gallery, after only a few months. He became one of the most famous theatre organists in the world, and always acknowledged the great help given him by Florence de Jong in the early days of his career at the New Gallery.

Foort joined the New Gallery in February 1926, with Florence Baga de Jong, as she was then known, continuing as Orchestral Organist, which meant that Foort did the solo spots including opening house (which he always hated), with Florence accompanying the silents with the orchestra, sometime solo. Reg. Foort recalls those days in his book, 'The Cinema Organ'. 'A few months later I began to broadcast and make gramophone records on this organ, and its instantaneous success was really remarkable. Here was something entirely new, an instrument that could play any kind of music in the world – cheerful or sad, symphonic or ballad, fox-trot or folk-song, in such a way that it could be thoroughly enjoyed by the 'man in the street'.

'An instrument – virtually an orchestra under the control of a single performer – with an extra-ordinary range of tone colours, complete with all the orchestral effects, drums and cymbals, glockenspiel and chimes, which was ideal for accompanying pictures and could be made to sound like a cathedral organ or reproduce with amazing rhythm the effect of a dance band, it is hardly to be wondered that the said 'man in the street' took it straight to his heart, and, whether

At the New Gallery Regent Street in 1925, Florence de Jong.

he listened to it in the theatre or it came to him through his wireless set, found it a thoroughly satisfying form of entertainment.

'The New Gallery organ (was) a new departure in the history of the cinema organ in England. Nothing like it had been heard before, and, from the moment that I began to accompany pictures on it and play it to the world at large through the medium of broadcasting and recording, it had a tremendous influence on the design of all the cinema organs installed since.'

When Florence told General Manager of the New Gallery that her little sister Ena's job had literally gone up in smoke, he told her to bring her to London to assist at the New Gallery. There was much hard work in the cinema on those days as every film was silent and required musical accompaniment. Most of the smaller cinemas could only afford the services of a pianist, sometimes augmented by a violinist and other, but some kind of musical background was essential, if only to drown the sometimes noisy audiences! A somewhat refined clientele patronised the New Gallery, and the accompaniment of films by both orchestra and organ had become a fine art at that establishment, as befitted its name. Ena, now aged 20, already had several years experience in film accompaniment first on piano and more recently at a pipe organ, and she now had the ideal situation in which to build on her early years and to become thoroughly experienced at the Wurlitzer.

Actually, James Swift, who later played a similar organ at the Grange Kilburn and went on to the Astoria Hull, Savoy Brighton and Paramounts at Leeds and Newcastle, had been tipped for the third post at the New Gallery. However, Bill

16

Evans, the Managing Director of Provincial Cinematograph Theatres and whose office was at the New Gallery, heard Florence and Ena playing together, and came down the aisle, saying 'What's this – the Dolly Sisters?' He asked Ena if she would like to work with her sister, and referred her to the Musical Director, Ernest Grimshaw. All was arranged.

By 1926, Florence's husband, Harry de Jong, had moved from the New Gallery to the Super, Charing Cross Road, for United Picture Theatres (which became a subsidiary of Gaumont-British in 1930) and the orchestra leader, at the New Gallery was Alfred Fyler. He was heard to say in a loud voice 'She plays better than the men', and Ena often felt in those days that her appointment as an orchestral organist at a West End Flagship at the age of 20 made some of the other organists envious.

Ena has always had an engaging personality and, although Florence was the real beauty of the family, all the daughters were attractive. Within a short time of her arrival at the New Gallery, Ena had received three offers of marriage. One from the Manager, Elliot Turnbull; one from the 'cellist in the orchestra; and one from the trombonist, whose name was Jacamole. He said 'You are so beautiful, you will make love to me while I play the trombone'. One can't help wondering if the slide might have got in the way! Eventually, Ena married the Manager, Elliot Turnbull.

While Florence and Harry were still living at Southend, they were blessed with a baby daughter, Pauline. Both became so busy in London that they put Pauline into the care of friends at Thundersley, about 6 miles from Southend. The friends looked after Pauline extremely well and taught her that she must always look both ways and be very careful crossing the busy, dangerous road on which they lived. One afternoon, when she was eight years of age, she begged to go and buy some sweets. Her view obstructed by a parked car, she was knocked down and instantly killed. Ena believes that the parents, Florence and Harry, blamed themselves for being preoccupied with their careers and that Florence never completely got over Pauline's death.

One of the first super cinemas in the UK was the Regent Brighton, designed by Robert Atkinson, who provided a superb plan to include 3,000 seats and a magnificent interior described as 'a robust Adamesque adaptation of Roman Classical motifs'. The Regent had two restaurants and a straight organ by Hill, Norman & Beard, played from 1923 to 1928 by Terance Casey. In the year that Casey began playing at the Regent, 1923, a new cinema opened on the south side of the Strand in London, close to Charing Cross Station and partly on the site of the old Tivoli Music Hall, from which it took its name. The old Tivoli was decorated in the Indian manner, and it has been said that it became so synonymous with variety that its style of decoration created a vogue that influenced music halls all over Britain. The old Tivoli had closed in 1914 and it was not until 9 years later that the new Tivoli Cinema, with its much simpler facade in Portland Stone, opened. It was acquired by MGM, but, in 1928, when they opened their new Empire in Leicester Square the Tivoli was taken over by PCT, providing a second West End outlet to the New Gallery. Within two weeks, PCT had installed a Wurlitzer, one rank larger than the New Gallery, with the chambers behind a grille where one of the boxes had been at the side of the procenium arch. Terance Casey came up from Brighton to open the Wurlitzer; Harry Fryer came from the PCT's Picture House Glasgow to be the Musical Director (with an orchestra of 22); and the lady appointed Assistant Organist came from the New Gallery – Ena Baga!

Describing the re-opening of the Tivoli on 27th November, 1928, the 'Melody Maker' said 'On the opening night Ernest Grimshaw, the Musical Adviser of the PCT conducted the orchestra with all his usual skill, and a very finished performance was given of the 'Robespierre' Overture. In the orchestral film accompaniment which followed the music was not only well chosen but exceedingly well played. Terance Casey presides at the Console of the new Wurlitzer organ and his fine playing is just as marked in the kinema as on his numerous records which were made from the New Gallery Organ, Regent Street. Miss Ena Baga (sister of Madam de Jong) is acting as Assistant Organist.' But, not for long!

In 1928 the famous London Palladium went over to films for about two to three months. One of 50 or more theatres belonging to the General Theatre Corporation, it had been taken over in March, 1928, with that circuit by PCT. who decided to try films. Surprising for such a well-known variety theatre, and even more surprising, a Model 'F' Wurlitzer was installed on the stage, with console in the orchestra pit. Reginald Foort moved over from the New Gallery, and his place as Solo Organist taken by Florence de Jong. When films ceased at the Palladium, the Wurlitzer was moved to the Plaza, Allerton, Liverpool, and both Mr. and Mrs. Foort went too! The organ was opened at Allerton by Reg Foort, with his wife playing the violin and with organist Bobby Pagan at the piano. Foort then went to the new Empire

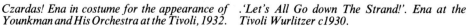

Czardas! Ena in costume for the appearance of Younkman and His Orchestra at the Tivoli, 1932.   *.'Let's All Go down The Strand!'. Ena at the Tivoli Wurlitzer c1930.*

Leicester Square, as Orchestral Organist with Sandy Macpherson as Solo, until 1929 when he opened the Regent Bournemouth, also for PCT. In 1930, he opened a Compton, designed by him, at the incredibly atmospheric New Victoria Cinema, followed by the Regal Marble Arch at the giant Christie in succession to Quentin Maclean. In 1932 he opened a beautiful Wurlitzer at the Regal Kingston-on-Thames, and from 1933 to 1936 he was Musical Director for County Cinemas, opening their Conacher theatre organs at Nottingham, Wimbledon, Margate, Hull and Southampton. After a short spell with Paramount at Tottenham Court Road, he was appointed Staff Organist to the BBC, in competition with some of the top names of the time, presiding at the new BBC Compton installed in the Variety Department's St. George's Hall, next to the Queen's Hall, Langham Place.

In a national competition organised by the Daily Express in 1937, Reginald Foort was voted THE Most Popular Broadcaster, ahead of Gracie Fields and Reginald Dixon! Nevertheless, he left the BBC in 1938 to tour the variety halls with his mammoth Möller theatre organ until wartime conditions made it impossible. In 1951 he sold the Möller to the BBC as a replacement for the St. George's Hall Compton lost in the blitz, and emigrated to the USA. He returned just once, twenty years later, for a concert tour. He died in 1980, aged 87, and one of the last messages he sent was one of greeting to Florence de Jong and Ena Baga, with whom he had worked more than fifty years previously at the New Gallery.

Back to 1928 and the Tivoli, where Ena was asked to play for a special film performance for naval cadets. Ena struck up with, appropriately, 'A Life On The Ocean Wave' and, thinking of shore leave, 'Home, Sweet, Home'. The Tivoli Manager came rushing down to the console, saying 'What are you doing? They're all orphans!'.

Just after the Tivoli opened, PCT amalgamated with the Gaumont- British Picture Corporation, which had been formed in March 1927 by the joining together of Biocolour Picture Theatres, the W.F. Film Service and the Gaumont Company, which had been launched in 1898 and had its origin with Leon Gaumont in France. Ena and Florence, therefore, were both employed by GB, a fast-expanding company with interests in both production and exhibition, and which within the next ten years controlled nearly 300 cinemas.

In 1929 the Regent Brighton, which had been damaged by a fire, reopened and Terance Casey went back, this time to open a new Wurlitzer. He remained with Gaumont-British for the next twenty years, at Chelsea, Haymarket (a rebuilding of the Capitol), the Trocadero Elephant & Castle, Gaumont State Kilburn and Gaumont Palace Hammersmith. After a spell of free-lancing including the RMS Queen Mary, he returned to the Gaumont Haymarket for a few years. One of his last appearances was at the Odeon Croydon in 1959, where he played preludes on a Compton Melotone organ for 'Around The World In Eighty Days', but he was obviously then not at his best. He died in 1972.

With Casey's departure from the Tivoli, Ena was appointed to succeed him, and she soon became popular there. Not long after she took over, a Midnight Matinee was staged,, with a painting to be auctioned for charity. The programme sellers were all debutantes and there was a star-studded cast, including Noel Coward, Gertrude Lawrence, Seymour Hicks, Ivy St. Helier and Evelyn Laye. Wearing the

Florence in Lloyd-Loom Chair at the New Gallery, 1932 (photo: Frank Buckingham).

usual dressing-gown and with the famous cigarette-holder, Noel Coward went down to Ena's room and asked her what she was going to play for the Matinee. 'Bitter Sweet', she answered. 'Oh, do you know it?' was Coward's reply. Noel and Gertie performed an excerpt from 'Private Lives', which had its première at the King's Theatre Edinburgh on 18th August 1930. As Sheridan Morley says in his excellent biography of Gertrude Lawrence, '. . . theirs was perhaps the definitive light-comedy partnership of the Century, and never better expressed than in this one play." Ena joined in the accompaniment to their immortal duet 'Some Day I'll Find You'. Evelyn Laye also sang a Noel Coward song, and Seymour Hicks auctioned the painting, even suggesting in which small room it could be hung!!

The old Tivoli Music Hall, built in 1888, had become the most famous of music halls, featuring the top names of the day such as Harry Tate, Bransby Williams, Dan Leno, Florrie Forde, George Robey, Eugene Stratton and Harry Lauder. The music hall atmosphere somehow clung on to the rebuilt theatre, and the management decided to stage cine-variety for one year, i.e. a blend of films and live acts. This kept Ena very busy, accompanying the 'Blue Hungarian Band', Macari and His Dutch Serenaders, and the American Ethel Waters, from 'On With The Show', who sang 'Dinah'. Ena recalls that Ethel Waters was very nervous and had not hitherto sung to an organ accompaniment. It went so well, that she tore her bouquet in two and presented half to Ena, as if to say 'half the success is due to you'.

Macari and His Dutch Serenaders appeared at the Croydon Empire in the late 1940s, by which time they had their own lady organist, the vivacious Elsey Moncks, who had her own 'spot', theatre organ style, in the middle of the act. We later met after she succeeded Ena and Doreen Chadwick at Lyons' Oxford Corner House in the 1950s, when she introduced me to her husband, David, also in the Macari Band. He later became famous as 'Dai' Francis, the Al Jolson-style singer with The Mitchell Minstrels!

'Showplace of the North'. Florence and Southan Morris examining plans for the Ritz Birkenhead in 1936.

CHAPTER FOUR

In 1932 came a milestone in Ena's life. She was invited to take part in the Royal Command performance of 'The Gold Rush' before King George V and Queen Mary at Balmoral. She stayed at the Invercauld Arms at Ballater about 8 miles from Balmoral Castle, and travelled up with Bill Thornton, the Tivoli Manager, and a representative from the United Artists Corporation named McFarlane. Three performances were given, beginning with a rehearsal, followed by the actual Royal Command and a performance for the children of the Royal Balmoral Estate. Ena's accompaniment to the film was entirely from memory, and she had a drummer with her for the effects. She remembers the Command performance as a glittering affair with kilts and a myriad of sparkling diamonds, and will ever carry in her mind the sight of the King nearly falling off his chair with laughter! At the end of the show, Ena was presented to the King and Queen, after which she went up to bed fairly exhausted!

She was of course unable to sleep from the excitement of it all, and after a while there came a knocking on her hotel bedroom door and a voice said 'Come and have some champagne'. Ena was still only 26 years of age, and she says that she was rather naïve and suffering from something of an inferiority complex. She did not dream that she would be invited to a champagne reception.

The Command Performance was fully reported in the Southend press, including the fact that her accompaniment was entirely from memory and supported only by a drummer and that she was personally congratulated by Their Majesties. The event was also carried by the Daily Sketch and the Daily Express, who published a photograph of Ena at the Tivoli console under the head-line 'PLAYED BEFORE THE KING'.

The Baga family were of course well-known in Southend from their music appearances, and the eldest daughter, Celeste, was resident at the Rivoli Cinema in the town. Indeed, Florence and Ena were beginning to make a name for themselves in the West End of London.

Not only was the Tivoli a very fine theatre, but it had a restaurant, two luncheon bars and a downstairs Dutch Buffet beneath the foyer. Ena met all kinds of people down there, including Tom Webster, the famous cartoonist. She says that each day he would get a little 'merry' and proceed to draw the next day's cartoon on the back of the Buffet Menu!

Meanwhile, Florence and Harry de Jong found the travelling from Southend rather too much and had taken a flat practically opposite the Super in Charing Cross Road, where Harry was Musical Director. As part of United Picture Theatres, the Super came under Gaumont-British management in 1930, becoming the Tatler News Theatre in 1931. Florence and Harry decided to buy a house at Wembley, and on the day they moved out of their flat a quite extraordinary thing happened. The most important thing to musicians is of course their grand piano, and just as it was being lowered on ropes from their flat to the removal van below,

Queen Mary drove up Charing Cross Road in an open carriage, and the piano was left suspended in mid-air until she had safely passed. History does not relate what she thought if she looked up, but she was not the only Queen Mary to figure in the lives of Florence and Ena, as we shall see.

While at the Tivoli, Ena had divorced her first husband, Elliott Turnbull, and remarried. Her second husband had the grand name of James Hamilton-Brown, and they took a flat at the back of the Tivoli in John Adam Street.

In the mid-thirties Ena began making recordings, the first (in March, 1935) for the Solex label, later transferred to Sterno, being piano solos. The first, couples 'Smoke Gets In Your Eyes' with Billy Mayerl's 'White Heather', and the second contains two selections – 'Kid Millions' and 'Road House'. While at the Tivoli, Ena used the obvious 'Let's All Go Down The Strand' as a signature tune, but later adopted 'Smoke Gets In Your Eyes', the lovely Jerome Kern ballad and the first piece she recorded. 'His Master's Voice' then introduced her to the ranks of the recording theatre organists with 'Moonlight Dance' and 'Marigold' (Billy Mayerl), strangely not at the Tivoli Wurlitzer but at the New Gallery.

In 1937, Gaumont-British introduced a policy of touring their organists, but the Tivoli remained as Ena's base theatre. In December 1937 she visited the Gaumont Bromley, which beautiful theatre had opened just over a year before with two feature films, a stage production entitled 'Trafalgar Square', Bobby Howell and His Band, and Terance Casey (Ena's former partner at the Tivoli) as guest organist from Chelsea. The cavernous interior, suggestive of a large shell with shell motifs, had 2,500 seats. The organ was under-stage and was a 10-rank Compton with 4 keyboards (manuals) and a clever Compton patent electronic unit that produced the most mellifluous sounds and known appropriately as the 'Melotone'. Ena thought this device very effective but that it should not be over-used and restricted to ballads and slow numbers. She thought the organ, which had a console on a lift to the left of the orchestra lift, a very nice instrument. During her week there, the Bromley Amateur Cup Final team made an appearance on stage, and the press reported 'Before and after their appearance the organist, Miss Ena Baga, played two of the clubs theme songs, appropriate words for which were thrown on the screen . . .'

On the Friday morning local children were entertained, and the Mayor and Mayoress of Bromley came along to judge a talent contest. D.M. Jackson Film Editor of the 'Bromley and West Kent Mercury' acted as Father Christmas, and he and Ena were photographed with the Mayor, Mayoress, a group of VAD members who helped with the entertainment, and Manager Alfred Watts, who Ena says was a very nice man. He later bought the Palais de Luxe in Bromley and ran that until his death in 1953.

Another lady who made a guest appearance at Bromley Gaumont in the following year was Molly Forbes. Born in Cardiff, she had begun piano lessons very early in life and gained her LRAM and ARM at the age of 18. Like Celeste, Florence and Ena, she had intended to make the piano her career but a friend, Al Bollington, who was with Paramount in London, urged her to take up the cinema organ. She joined Gaumont-British as Assistant to Fredric Bayco at the GB Flagship, the Dominion Tottenham Court Road, in 1937, then as relief organist to

Everyone loves a fair lady when she's 40. Florence in 1937.

Ena at the Tivoli and Florence at the New Gallery. By 1937, Florence had completed nearly 13 years at the New Gallery and, although popular, felt that it was time for a change. Someone then came into her life who would make that change, and who would have a great effect on her career.

Born in East London and as a child described as 'a pocket edition of Eddie Cantor, with an ever-ready smile – a smile which gave him a "lift" to Good Fortune', Lou Morris was only 'knee-high to a grasshopper' when he asked a local coke merchant for a job. He showed great enterprise at the age of nine by purchasing a magic lantern and giving shows to local children in his parents' cellar for a farthing! At twelve, he took a job in a coal mine in South Wales, working 12 hours a night for the princely sum of two shillings! After twelve years, as Foreman, he took a holiday in London and joined a relative who ran a cinema, becoming Assistant Manager. Six months later, Lou was running his own cinema and, seeing a need for bigger and better buildings in new, developing areas, he built the first cinema with provision for car-parking, a wise decision that was to pay dividends. By 1935, he had built, or rebuilt, about 30 cinemas and owned two Rolls-Royce cars!

You will remember that Lou Morris had met the Baga family and had, years earlier, wished to marry Celeste. Upon visiting the New Gallery, Lou was captivated by the charm and ability of the lady organist, Florence de Jong, and was determined to present her at his theatres. Needing a change, Florence agreed to join his company. Before doing so, there was one more important function she had to perform at the New Gallery and this was to play for the Royal Première of 'Doctor Syn' with George Arliss, Margaret Lockwood and John Loder, before Her Majesty Queen Mary, on November 10th, 1937. So, both younger sisters had appeared before Royalty, one by Royal Command and the other at a Royal Première!

Meanwhile, Ena was still making guest appearances from her base at the Tivoli. In May, 1938, a special concert was held at the Regent Sheffield in aid of the Markham Colliery Fund, with Jessie Matthews at the top of the bill, introduced by husband, Sonnie Hale. The programme began with Peter Kilby at the Wurlitzer, resident organist at the theatre, followed by the Sheffield Empire Theatre Orchestra, four supporting acts and then, special guest organist Ena Baga. Ena played a selection of songs from Gilbert & Sullivan operas, followed by the Russian 'Black Eyes'. She stayed at the console to accompany Jessie Matthews in 'The Natural Thing To Do', 'Dearest Heart' and, in response to loud requests from the audience her hit song from 1937, 'Gangway'. Jessie Matthews received a tremendous ovation, but Ena recalls that she was terribly nervous at making a personal appearance, pacing the wings beforehand and rushing off stage at one point before recovering her poise and confidence! Ena stayed for the week at Sheffield and very much liked the Model F Wurlitzer, which dated from 1927. Unhappily it was removed from the Regent in 1962.

While in Sheffield, Ena and husband Jim met up with Jim's Uncle Sid at the Grand Hotel. Encouraged by the two men, Ena drank several Pimms', she forgets how many, and found that her legs would not work when it came time to leave!

Florence was actually the first lady to make a theatre organ broadcast at the BBC

The first lady to broadcast from the BBC Theatre Organ. Florence at the St. George's Hall Compton in 1938.

Compton, a superb instrument of 23 ranks on 4 manuals, with 'phantom' grand piano playable from the console, and Melotone Unit. It was housed in St. George's Hall, Langham Place, used by the BBC Variety Department and previously leased by the Maskelyne family of magical fame. The organ was opened in 1936 by Quentin Maclean, Harold Ramsay, Reginald Foort and Reginald Porter-Brown. Ena speedily followed Florence with a broadcast on January 19th, 1938, her first. The third lady to gain an airing was Peggy Weber, who had begun her career at the Kingsway Hadleigh (near the Baga family home at Southend) at the age of eighteen. Following a short spell touring the country with Harold Ramsay as the 'Radio Rodeo' organist, Peggy was appointed to the Odeon Weston-Super-Mare in August, 1938 whence she continued to broadcast.

Other places visited by Ena were the New Victoria Bradford, which had a 10-rank Wurlitzer in chambers above the stage, which, in a 3,300-seat theatre could hardly be heard. It had to be amplified. Mr. Ridley, the Manager of the New Victoria, took Ena to see Ilkley Moor. Forgetting to apply the hand-brake, they had to chase the car over the moors, Mr. Ridley's big ears 'flapping in the wind'. At the New Cross Cinema which to theatre organists was like the Glasgow Empire to English comedians, Ena tried a selection of hits by Fred Astaire. There was no response whatever from the audience, so the thought to herself 'I'll make you applaud'. For the second interlude, she tried a Latin-American selection, finishing with 'Tico-Tico'. They actually clapped, enthusiastically!

27

At the Regal Edmonton, with its Christie opened by Sidney Torch, the lift used to shake frighteningly; Ena liked both the Wurlitzers at Stamford Hill and Bournemouth, the latter having been opened by Foort in 1929.

Another theatre she visited was the Grange Kilburn, with a Model 'F' Wurlitzer like the New Gallery; and the Trocadero Elephant & Castle, where she deputised for the great Quentin Maclean. With Mac's enormous popularity in the New Kent Road, he was very difficult to stand-in for, but 'with a little bit of this and a little of that', she says she got a very good reception. At the Ambassador, Hendon, she deputised for G.T. Pattman, who early in his career had toured the halls with a travelling pipe organ. Pattman was really a concert organist with a leaning towards 'straight' music, but from 1922 to 1934, he went around opening cinema organs, never staying for very long! He opened the Super Ilford, Pavilion Shepherd's Bush, Capitol Haymarket, Kings Cross Cinema, Central Sheffield, Astoria Charing Cross Road, Pavilion Wigan, Palace Slough, Astorias at Brixton and Finsbury Park, and the Forum Ealing, all in the space of twelve years. Ena says he used to get away with Bach fugues at Hendon!

In July 1938 Ena appeared at the Gaumont Finchley, sharing the bill with Shirley Temple ('Rebecca of Sunnybrook Farm') and playing an excellent Compton, removed in 1967 to The Plough Inn, Great Munden, Hertfordshire, where (in 1993) she still appears regularly, the only theatre pipe organ in a pub in the world!

On visiting the Gaumont Camden Town, where there was another very fine Compton, the Manager told her that the resident organist, Con Docherty, was leaving. Ena was living at Chalk Farm nearby, so, when asked if she would like to make Camden Town her base, she readily agreed. Con Docherty had begun his career as relief pianist and organist at the Queen's Hall Newcastle, followed by the New Coliseum Whitley Bay. In 1933 he came to London, to the Queen's Hall Cricklewood, then opened the Gaumont Palace Derby and Gaumont Ashton-Under-Lyne, before taking the residency at Camden Town in 1937. He then went to Gaumonts at Finchley and Lewisham, and after the war at Doncaster and the Paramount/Odeon Newcastle. In 1955 he transferred to management of theatres for Rank. In the late 1980s he could be found playing an electronic organ at the Top Rank Club Gateshead, and he appeared as the 'mystery guest' in 'What's My Line' at a Gunton Hall Organ Week End.

Cine-variety was the order of the day at Camden Town, and Ena accompanied top-of-the-bill stars like Jimmy Edwards, Adelaide Hall, Vic Oliver and Semprini. For as little as 9d in old currency, one could see a second feature, followed by Gaumont-British News (with its distinctive opening march 'Music From The Movies' by Louis Levy and the Gaumont British Symphony), a cartoon, organ interlude, the main feature and one hour's variety. What value for money!

Instead of rising on a lift in the conventional manner, the console at Camden Town slid out of an alcove in the wall to the edge of the stage, and could be made to revolve. A drop festoon curtain, heavily weighted, covered the alcove, and this rose and fell as the console appeared and departed. One evening the curtain fell too quickly, and would have 'crowned' Ena had she not jumped off the console. Another minor catastrophy was when one of the orchestra took a friend into the pit and the friend accidentally trod onto the conductor's button to raise the orchestra lift. All the instruments and music-stands rose in front of the screen in the middle of the big picture!

There was very little time for meal-breaks, but there was a 'marvellous little pub' at the rear of the Gaumont, where for 1/- one could enjoy 'joint and two veg.' and sweet, and all the artists went there. At this time, Ena's sister Beatrice and her husband moved to Kingston-on-Thames, and Ena had as neighbour on the top floor, Walter Landauer. She used to go up and play piano duets with him!

Just after Christmas, 1938, Ena was invited to go to Stanford Hall, Loughborough, to take part in the first public entertainment staged there by Sir Julien Cahn. The big surprise at the 18th Century Stanford Hall is the private theatre built by Sir Julien so that he could demonstrate his knowledge of the art of magic. Outwardly, the building looks like a wing added to match the period but, inside, one is amazed to find a fully-equipped theatre/cinema to 1930s modern design, complete with trough lighting, orchestra pit and Wurlitzer organ with the console on a lift! As the local reporter said on that night, 'amazement was divided between the host's perplexing magic and the truly unique setting.' The audience at one point whispered various operatic excerpts to their host, and a 'super-natural' gramophone played the tunes. The show was made up with ballet and speciality dancing, an Australian entertainer, xylophone solos and Ena Baga at the Wurlitzer. The local press carried a picture of Ena bowing to plaudits from the console. Stanford Hall is now a college, but the theatre is used by local groups and the Wurlitzer sounds as sweet as ever. The only thing missing is the automatic player, transferred to The Musical Museum at Brentford.

Ignoring Ena's performance, the press said 'The organ, by the way, is the only one in the country that plays itself'!

Six months after Ena had transferred to Camden Town, a very nice tribute was paid to her in the St. Pancras Chronicle. A young Irish violinist, Tamara MacInnery, made a professional appearance at the Gaumont, at the age of 19. She played the Intermezzo from 'Cavalleria Rusticana' and the 'Londonderry Air'. 'The success of the performance', said the press, 'was greatly enhanced by Miss Ena Baga's sympathetic accompaniment on the big organ'.

Madame Arcana, prophet of Radio Pictorial, had predicted that organists Fredric Bayco and Ena Baga would be successful as radio stars. In April, 1939, she pointed how her predictions had come true, Bayco being one of the most regular and popular broadcasting cinema organists, and Ena having made seven broadcasts on the BBC Theatre Organ and having been honoured with Command Performances at Balmoral and at Lady Mountbatten's home before the King of Spain. But, even greater things were to follow!

In the heyday of the theatre organ in the UK, there were roughly 500 theatre organists. Only about one-tenth were ladies, and one wonder what it felt like to be a star in what was essentially a man's world? Ena says that the sisters all earned a good living because of their talent. Celeste was a brilliant sight-reader, essential for accompanying variety acts (cine-variety was very much the vogue in the 1930s, particularly on the Union and Gaumont-British circuits). It obviously helped if the management were well disposed towards their organists (they were not always!),

Florence comes to Finchley! Two feature films plus a guest organist at the Gaumont Finchley; and tea afterwards in the restaurant. Florence can be seen below the 'N' of Gaumont. c1937 (photo by G.C. Crispin).

and Ena says that Bill Evans at the New Gallery was very fond of Florence. Ena says that the male organists were all quite courteous, even if some of them may have been envious of Florence and Ena's positions in the West End. The attitude towards women taking up a profession in the 1930s, rather than staying at home, is quite different from what it is today, and the Second-world-war contributed to that. As the male organists were called up, so the ladies took their places and some of the plum jobs, e.g. the Tower Blackpool and the Warner Leicester Square were occupied by females. It seems wrong in retrospect that this could only happen in a state of emergency, but then one remembers that the Baga sisters had broken into the West End of London in 1925.

Travelling may have been one of the reasons why the ladies were not attracted in large numbers. Although the private cinemas tended to have a resident organist, sometimes covering more than one theatre, circuits like Union and Granada toured their organists and, as we have seen, Gaumont-British liked theirs to make guest appearances around the UK. Long absences play havoc with home life and can even wreck marriages. Ena's first husband was a cinema manager and was out all day long, whereas Florence's husband Harry de Jong worked cinema hours like herself. Ena says that Beatrice's husband, Christian Palle, adored her and did not mind how much she was away from home on engagements. All the husbands knew they were marrying musicians who would have to do much travelling, and in most cases the husbands were in the business themselves. Molly Forbes, for example, met her husband at an ABC cinema where he was a manager, but in later years the travelling did get her down and she was quite glad to leave ABC in the mid-fifties. Ena says that, once she was free of domestic commitments, she loved travelling – as she did, around the world.

CHAPTER FIVE

On Sunday November 7th, Reginald Foort had presided at the Gala Opening of the Compton organ at Lou Morris's latest theatre, the Regal, Guernsey, in the Channel Islands. The theatre, the only super cinema in the island of Guernsey, had actually opened on the 31st May, but for some reason the organ followed nearly six months' afterwards. It was an 8-rank Compton instrument, and the 3-manual console had what was known as the 'Rainbow' style of illuminated surround. Foort performed twice on the opening day, such was the demand for tickets, and his programme ranged from the Zampa overture and 'Reminiscences of Chopin' to 'In a Monastry Garden' and 'Popular Hits of the Moment'. Reginald Foort was BBC Staff Organist at that time, and the programme for the Gala Concert mentioned that in 1937 he had made 115 solo broadcasts and 24 transmissions to the Empire, had been on the air for nearly 100 hours and had played 1,000 tunes!

By the beginning of 1938, Lou Morris controlled a dozen cinemas up and down the country, although he had disposed of one or two. He acquired cinemas in London at Bow and Willesden, at Chesham, Boscombe, Margate, Didsbury, Wembley, Norwich (the Carlton, which he rebuilt) Harrow, and Bridgnorth. Apart from Guernsey, he had built the Princess Dagenham in 1932 (at the request of Henry Ford & Co, according to Florence), Playhouse Dewsbury in 1931, and the Plaza theatres at Sutton and Worthing in 1934. Dewsbury and Worthing had both been taken over by ABC, and the Plaza Sutton was acquired by Granada, who already had an interest in it and were staffing it. In 1936, Lou had turned his attention to Northern Ireland and began building a large Ritz in Belfast. This was acquired by Union Cinemas during construction, and their M.D. Harold Ramsay ensured that the Compton (ordered by Lou Morris) was an absolute stunner!

Also in 1936, Lou commissioned two schemes for Watford from the Norwich architect J.Owen Bond, one for North Watford to be known as the Ritz, and one for Watford High Street, to be the Capitol. Before either got off the ground, Odeon had taken over the North Watford project and the Hyams Brothers (jointly with Gaumont-British) had bought the High Street plan for a State, which opened as the Gaumont! However, Lou did continue to build cinemas; in 1938 opening new Regals at Walton-on-Thames, Bridlington and Loftus, and a Ritz at Sheerness, on the Isle of Sheppey. He was very organ-minded, and installed 8-rank Comptons at Walton and Bridlington, opened by Reginald Foort and Florence de Jong respectively.

It was planned to have an organ at Sheerness, but before this was ordered, Lou and Florence were invited to the Acton works of the John Compton Organ Company to hear their new invention, a complete organ that was electronic and developed from their successful Melotone Unit. It was to be called the 'Theatrone', and Lou and Florence were so impressed with its tonal quality and compactness that they decided there and then to buy one. And so it was that one of the first Compton Theatrone 'pipeless' organs was installed at the Ritz Sheerness, to be opened by Florence de Jong. The first models had most attractive eliptical-shaped consoles, and it is at one of these that we picture Florence at the Ritz Sheerness. Later Theatrones installed in cinemas, such as the Apollo Ardwick and Regal Darlaston had full-size consoles and looked similar to theatre pipe organs. That at Ardwick was soon replaced with a Compton pipe organ.

Lou was particularly proud of his Regal Bridlington, virtually a twin to that at Walton-on-Thames, both theatres being by the same architect, with similar auditoria and large café restaurants. In August 1939, Ena took some holiday from her base at Camden Town and joined Florence, Celeste and Beatrice for a special presentation at Bridlington called 'Bag'a Tricks' featuring the organ, two pianos and violin. The Bridlington Free Press went to town on what they described as an 'excellent and novel presentation', and, as it reports in detail what was obviously a unique and outstanding entertainment by the Baga family, it is worth reproducing here.

'The Regal Cinema management is to be congratulated on its excellent and novel presentation of Florence de Jong and her three sisters, Celeste, Ena and Beatrice Baga at the cinema this week . . . All famous broadcasters, the sisters proved amazingly versatile. The opening number, 'Straussina', with Celeste and Ena at two pianos and Florence de Jong at the organ, was followed by 'No, No, Nanettee',

Florence lays a brick at the Ritz Birkenhead, watched by entrepreneur, Southan Morris. Described at the 'Showplace of the North', the Ritz was opened by Gracie Fields in October 1937. (photo: Wm Cull, Pictorial Press agency)

Visiting her sister's theatre! Florence at the Gaumont Camden Town in July, 1938. (photo by Tunbridge).

a piano duet by Celeste and Ena. Beatrice then followed with a violin solo, Monti's 'Czardas', after which she gave an encore, Tosselli's 'Serenata'.

'Ena then took the organ seat for two or three grand numbers, after which Celeste entertained at the piano with two selections, 'Three Blind Mice' and 'Kitten on the Keys'. An ensemble (a special arrangement of 'Boomps-a-Daisy') then followed, after which the four sisters led the audience, who were invited to join in the singing of several 'hits' of the year, including the popular 'South of the Border'. The climax was interposed with special slides. The lighting effects during the whole of this enjoyable half-hour were exceptionally effectively carried out.

'It is understood that Florence de Jong and her sisters are to be booked at several theatres in the near future. It is certain that wherever they appear they will receive ovations equal to those they have received this week . . .'

Following the opening of the Regal Guernsey Compton by Reginald Foort in November, 1937, Herbert Dowson was appointed resident organist. A church organist at the age of 14, Herbert Dowson became one of the pioneers of film accompaniment, playing a Jardine 'straight' organ at the Tivoli, Strand, just before Ena's Wurlitzer was installed in 1928. He played a similar instrument at the County Lancaster (conversion of the Hippodrome Theatre, which was a former Temperance Hall of 1859 and before that a Roman Catholic Chapel of 1799; after years of dereliction, now beautifully restored) until 1929. He was then employed by the John Compton Company to open their new organs at Handsworth (Birmingham), Luton, Nottingham, Southport and Kentish Town, before becoming resident at the Paramount Glasgow. A regular broadcaster, he was described as a talented musician who welcomed request items to build up his interludes. He came to Guernsey after a short spell at the newly-opened Westover Bournemouth, but in 1938 he went back to Southport, to open the Grand, and then began demonstrating the new Compton Theatrone electronic organs in Scotland.

The Regal then embarked on a long series of guest appearances by well-known organists, including Sunday concerts that were relayed to the Victoria, Town and Country Hospitals on the Island, the programme proceeds being devoted to the Victoria. Those featured in 1938 were Reginald Foort, Florence de Jong (with a direct line broadcast on March 12th), Harold Ramsay, Leslie James, F. Rowland Tims, Florence again (in July), Tommy Dando, Florence again (in August), Robinson Cleaver, Foort again, and, on December 11th, Reginald Porter-Brown. The organists were engaged to appear for the week following the Sunday concerts, and this arrangement continued into 1939, with Leslie James (and Glyn Davies, Boy Vocalist), John Madin, Dudley Beaven, Florence, and Robinson Cleaver making a return visit for a week commencing 16th July. Presumably, the organists arranged to take leave from their various cinema posts, and the delightful island of Guernsey would be ideal for a (working) holiday! The last two advertised were for August 20th, Cecil Chadwick, and September 17th Sandy Macpherson, and one would assume, with war being declared on September 3rd, that Sandy's two days of concerts would have been the Grand Finale until further notice!

However, one would reckon without a courageous lady!

'It is appropriate' said Mr. Eric Snelling, introducing London's leading lady organist to a crowded theatre at the Regal last night, 'that the first visiting organist

His latest creation! Lou Morris at the Ritz Sheerness, which he opened in 1938. (photo: Robert Gee)

since the outbreak of war should be a lady. For such talented women entertainers are, as in the last war, doing their bit for the country by keeping everyone happy on the Home Front.' So reported the Guernsey 'Star' on the welcoming introduction by the Manager of the Regal at Ena's opening night on Sunday October 29th, 1939. 'Hitler and the States', continued the Manager, 'had dimmed the Island's attractiveness for Ena Baga, but, despite this, she has braved a rough Channel crossing to play before the Regal's appreciative audiences.' In fact, Ena was very apprehensive as the boat left Jersey, as she had heard how rough it could be between the Islands. Seeing her expression, a tomato-grower on board advised her to stay on deck – but in the centre of the boat – and she arrived looking happy and as brown as a berry! On the return trip an enormous plane suddenly dived out of the sky and Ena prepared to say her final prayer. However, an Advocate from Guernsey travelling back to England with her reassured her that it was 'one of ours' protecting a convoy!

On August 8th, 1940, the Nazi air attacks on Britain began, first on the coastal cities, then inland airfields and aircraft factories, and then, from early September, the mass attack on London. Ena, still based at at the Gaumont Camden Town, slept at the theatre for several nights during the height of the blitz on London.

The back of the Gaumont was damaged and the theatre had to close for some time, so Ena was without a job. Bombed out, she did some piano-playing during the blitz at the Lyric Club, Shaftesbury Avenue. There was what Ena described as a 'screaming soprano' at the Club, who used to have hysterics when the bombing

The first of the few! Only a handful of electronic organs were installed in cinemas, but here is Florence at the Compton Theatrone at the Ritz Sheerness in 1938.

intensifed. Taxi-drivers used to join the artists and staff in the cellar of Stag & Russell's, drapers, in Leicester Square, during the air raids. Ena woke one night and thought that London was being gassed, but it turned out to be pair of neighbouring unwashed feet!

Meanwhile, Florence had been resident organist at the Regal Bridlington since early 1939, with guest appearances at the Regal Walton-on-Thames, where Lewis Gerard was resident; the Regal Guernsey; and the Ritz Sheerness, where Tommy Dando had guested for five weeks soon after the opening. 'Dando', as he was billed, had first played for silent films in Manchester and Bolton. His first theatre organ posts were at Eccles and Didsbury in the early thirties, coming south to open the Plaza Worthing for Lou Morris in 1934. From Worthing he moved to the Regal Rotherham, which theatre was leased by Lou from the Directors (and builders), Thos. Wade and his four sons. Dando returned to Rotherham, where he was very popular after his short stint at Sheerness, joining Gaumont-British in 1940, Granada in 1941, and returning to GB at the Gaumont Watford in 1944. CMA, who controlled both Gaumont and Odeon from 1948, sent him to their new theatre in Cairo, and from 1951, he went to Dublin, to the Savoy and finally the Theatre Royal, where he accompanied cine-variety. 'Dando' was very entertaining at the console and full of fun. He is still remembered in Rotherham with great affection.

In 1940, for a few months, the four sisters got together and toured Lou Morris' theatres with their superb act, 'Bag'a Tricks', and a series of these programmes was relayed by the BBC from Bristol. Florence opened the final Lou Morris cinema to be built, the Ritz at Grays, Essex, where there was already competition from Frederick's Electric Theatres (Abrahams) in the shape of an Empire,

Trying not to drop a brick are Florence and Reginald Foort at a topping-out ceremony with Lous Morris at his new theatre, the Regal, Loftus, Yorks.

Regal and, built in 1938, State, with combined seating for over 4,000! Lou added a further 1,500, but the Ritz only just managed to get its roof on as the war was starting! The organ opened by Florence was a Lafleur electronic, using the Hammond tone-wheel system, with the console on stage. Sister Celeste appeared there shortly afterwards and was blown off the console one night when a bomb landed just behind the theatre. Badly shaken, she bravely climbed back and, to boost the morale of the audience, struck up with 'There'll Always Be An England'!

And as if Hitler had heard of the great war-work the Baga sisters were doing to bolster up our spirits in those difficult days, another incident occured a short while afterwards, this time involving both Celeste and Ena. Ena had a broadcast arranged from the BBC Theatre Organ in St. George's Hall. Celeste came to meet her at the hall, and they discovered that due to the emergency situation, all transmissions for that evening had been cancelled except hers! She was warned that, as St. George's Hall had a glass roof, if she heard the alert she must run – fast! The broadcast went without a hitch, and, skirting part of the Langham Hotel that was lying in the street, the two sisters made their way to the Concert Hall in Broadcasting House ('BH' as it is affectionately known in the BBC) where a jazz-band programme was being transmitted. They slept in the Concert Hall that night, the ladies on one side and the men on the other, with a curtain in between. When they emerged next morning, it was to find that both the Queen's Hall and the adjacent St. George's had gone up in smoke! Florence was the first lady to broadcast on that celebrated organ. Ena was the last!

Broadcasts continued, on a Hammond electronic at Wood Norton, a country house the BBC had acquired near Evesham. A beautiful spot, as I discovered when on a week-end seminar there some forty years later! Going to 'Hog's Norton', as Ena always called it, she missed her intended train and arrived in the black-out. She saw a man in a bar wearing a fez, and, thinking that he would be connected with broadcasting (why else would a man in Worcestershire be wearing a fez?), she asked how she could get to the BBC. It turned out that he was nothing to do with the BBC at all, and Ena never did discover why he was wearing that fez! She managed to get a bus to the gates of Wood Norton, and, knowing that she was in the heart of the countryside, risked shining a torch to discover her whereabouts. A voice shouted 'Put that light out'. Having lost her way up the drive and fallen into the bushes, she was finally shown into the chapel, where there was a Model E Hammond, with ten minutes' to spare!

Harry de Jong had always loved the countryside, and at the outbreak of war he was given a post managing a cinema for Lou Morris, the Regal at Loftus, between Whitby and Redcar on the Yorkshire coast (now in Cleveland). Relatively speaking, it was not too far from Bridlington where Florence was based, but it was far enough. Sadly, Florence was obliged to divorce Harry but, although by that time Lou had obviously fallen in love with, and idolised her, it says much for Florence's 'Leo' principals and their self-discipline that they denied themselves any kind of relationship while she and Harry were still married. Set free, she was able to become Mrs. Lou Morris.

You may remember the West End Cinema Theatre that I mentioned earlier, opened in 1913 above the Elysee Restaurant, later the Café de Paris. As the Rialto, it was damaged by a bomb in March 1941, which exploded in front of the band-stand at the Café de Paris, killing Ken 'Snakehips' Johnson, the tenor-sax player and thirty-two customers. Sixty were seriously injured. Only a short while before, 'Snakehips' Johnson had taken part in a Jazz Jamboree at the Gaumont-State Kilburn in aid of the Musicians Benevolent Fund, with Ambrose, Geraldo, Jack Harris, George Melachrino, Sid Philips, Oscar Rabin, Al Bowlly and Sidney Torch! Lou took over the Rialto, patching it up and re-opening it in September 1942, with the Compton Theatrone from the Ritz Sheerness and guess who at the console? Florence de Jong; of course.

Mr and Mrs Lou Morris – just married.

CHAPTER SIX

Florence was now based at the Rialto Coventry Street and playing at other Lou Morris theatres. Celeste and Beatrice had teemed up together as the Baga Sisters, and were touring factories, appearing in such shows as 'Workers' Playtime', and they continued in this vogue for the duration. Molly Forbes had followed Ena at the Tivoli in 1938, also making guest appearances at other GB theatres including the Trocadero Elephant & Castle and the Regal Edmonton. In 1939, Al Bollington enlisted in the RAF, and Molly took his place at the superb Compton at the Paramount Tottenham Court Road, an organ well-known for Al's Broadcasts and recordings, both solo and with Anton & The Paramount Theatre Orchestra which had proved to be an excellent combination. In 1941, Phil Finch was called up from the Warner Theatre, and Molly took his place. The girls were therefore busy with their professional war-work, but what about Ena?

Visiting Evesham for a broadcast, Ena told Sandy Macpherson that she had been blitzed out of Camden Town and needed a job. Sandy replied that the Blackpool organists, Reginald Dixon and Horace Finch, had been called-up, and advised her to apply. An audition was arranged at the Opera House, which had been rebuilt in 1939, as part of the Winter Garden complex that also housed the Empress Ballroom. This was the third Opera House on this site and boasted a large stage (60 feet deep), dressing-rooms for more than 200, nearly 3,000 seats in the auditorium and the last Wurlitzer to be installed in the UK (apart from the Granada Kingston, which was a transfer). The specification of all three of the Tower Company's Wurlitzers was similar, except that the Tower was larger. The original Tower Wurlitzer of 1929, a 10-rank instrument, was transferred to the Empress Ballroom in the Winter Garden in 1935 and enlarged to 13 ranks and 3 manuals. (The Tower received a new 3/13 as a replacement, later enlarged). The Opera House Wurlitzer, opened by Reginald Dixon and Horace Finch in July 1939, differed from the Empress Wurlitzer in that it had more powerful strings (Gamba and Gamba Celeste), a tuba mirabilis in place of the Empress' nasal reed, the kinura, and, instead of a second tibia as at both the Empress and the Tower, the Opera House had a distinctive 'tibia plena', one of only two in the United Kingdom.

Following the audition, Ena returned to London as she was anxious about her parents, who were still living in Southend, which in 1940 was obviously a danger zone. I quote from 'The British People at War' – 'When the resistance of France collapsed and the British Expeditionary Force was evacuated from Dunkirk, the invasion of Britain became a very real menace. The Nation had long rested in a sense of security. Her reliance on the protection afforded by the sea had been implicit. Now, as in the Napoleonic days, the coasts must be manned. Watch and ward against assaults by airborne troops must be kept. An immediate sign of these preparations was the disappearance of anything that might guide an invader on his arrival. Gangs of men were seen removing road signs, painting out place-names on public buildings, hoardings and placards. Travellers by train were disconcerted by the anonymity of the stations through which they passed. Ways to the sea were barred, and those who, for sufficient reason, were allowed access to coastal areas were enjoined to walk warily.'

Elderly persons and children were advised to leave coastal areas in the South-East and East of Britain, and Ena made arrangements for her mother and father to stay with a friend, Clara Jacobs, who had a spare room at Edgware, Middlesex. Mama and Papa Baga didn't want to leave Southend, where they had lived for nearly twenty-five years (ironically, they had moved there from London during the First World War!), and Ena had a job to persuade them. Her husband, Jim, was in the Air Force, and Ena had to hire a van and move her parents and some of their possessions to Edgware. By a stark coincidence, their first night at Edgware was marred by heavy bombing – for the first time – and the next day they insisted upon returning to Southend-on-Sea! They had a shelter in the cellar there, so at least they would be reasonably safe from bombing!

Meanwhile, guest appearances at the Regal Bridlington had continued, where Ena was billed as 'The flippant-fingered personality girl' and 'London's Leading Lady Organist', appearing with such current films as 'the Stars Look Down' with Michael Redgrave and Margaret Lockwood; 'The Awful Truth' with Cary Grant and Irene Dunne; and 'The Black Room', with Boris Karloff. Patrons were entreated to see Ena Baga, 'retained for a further week at the Compton organ', also 'Karloff the terrible, Karloff the fiend, Karloff the monster''. With so many special freight and troop trains, normal rail schedules were disrupted, and the films were frequently delayed. The Bridlington press reported 'A novel interlude by Ena Baga at the Compton organ and Mr. G.H. Carlton on drums brought the Regal Cinema through a dilemma on Monday night. In the great rail hold-up, films due to be shown had not arrived, and the afternoon run of the programme had to be cancelled. At 6 o'clock the doors were opened as usual for the evening performances, although the films had still not arrived. The audience took the delay in good part and joined heartily in the community singing with Miss Baga at the organ, and then Mr. Carlton, the Regal manager, joined in with his drums. A short comedy was shown and at seven o'clock it was learned that the train by which the films were coming was still at Market Weighton.' Some thirty miles away! The report continued 'Miss Baga then played her selection which she had originally arranged for the evening performance. The films arrived about 7.30 p.m. and coincidentally the programme commenced almost exactly on the time scheduled for the last run of the evening. Another coincidence was Miss Baga repaid a debt she owed from the previous Monday, when she was unable to arrive in time for her first appearance at the organ.'

Broadcasting also continued, Ena being the first lady organist to broadcast 'For The Forces', on January 21st at 10.45 p.m. On February 5th, again 'For The Forces', Sandy Macpherson, who had succeeded Reginald Foort as BBC Staff Organist in 1938, arranged and presented a programme from the BBC Theatre Organ called 'Ladies' Night', with Ena (organ), Patricia Rossborough (piano) and vocalists Phyllis Robins and Esther Coleman. In April, Ena at the piano was joined by Florence at the organ and Celeste at another piano in a programme by 'The

Regal Trio', which I suspect was relayed from Bridlington, but the 'Radio Times' was censoring the source of outside broadcasts at that time. At the end of June, the Home Service repeated 'Bag'a Tricks' but this time with only three of the sisters, Florence (organ), Ena and Celeste (pianos), joined by Lionel Robbins (guitar) and vocalists Josephine Driver and Walter Midgley. In September, there was a further 'Bag'a Tricks' with the same cast, and another at the end of that month but without the guitarist and John Duncan in place of Walter Midgley. In January 1941, Ena played 'Music While You Work' at 10.30 in the morning, opening and closing with the programme's signature tune, 'Calling All Workers' by Eric Coates. The majority of these programmes, broadcast both morning and afternoon 'For The Forces', featured orchestras and small instrumental groups, but many were played by organists and the first one of all was by Dudley Beaven, who had been drafted in to assist Sandy at the outbreak of hostilities.

Dudley Beaven had begun his career in 1929 by opening a small Compton at the Cameo Charing Cross Road, followed by five years at the incredibly 'atmospheric' New Victoria cinema. In 1936 he joined Granada, opening their theatres at Greenford and Slough. In 1946 he suffered a nasty accident, fracturing his left leg and injuring his right foot. Depressed, perhaps from the anxiety that he might not be able to play again, he tragically took his own life. A terrible loss of a very fine organist!

Early in 1941, Ena was called to Blackpool to take up her post at the Tower Ballroom, in succession to Reginald Dixon. Although she had an appointment with the Musical Adviser of the Tower Company, Frank Jepson, her train was inevitably late and the appointment was missed. Blackpool in January was cold and dark, although it was full of servicemen and women, and civil servants. She asked the taxi-driver if she could find a bed for the night, and the place he took her to was full of 'dizzy blondes and Polish Officers'. Ena says that the bed-linen did not look too clean, but she was conducted to a reasonably clean room on the top floor, and she made sure there was a lock on the door! At breakfast there was a large thumb-mark on her plate!

Ena met Mr. Jepson the next day in the Tower Restaurant, in somewhat of a state, but he told her to calm down and to stay at the boarding house for just one further night. It turned out that the place where Ena was staying was something of a brothel, so Jepson told her – trying not to laugh! Hearing music coming from a small hotel, 'The Bentley' at North Shore, Ena rang the bell. An elderly woman answered, wearing a deaf-aid, so Ena shouted to her that she was a 'wandering minstrel' and must find somewhere to live. The owner, the woman's son, turned out to be a former cornet player from Willenhall in the West Midlands, with a strong Black Country accent. Ena told him about her appointment at the Tower, and he consented to give her a room. He was such a brass band enthusiast that he never missed a concert on the radio, which he would listen to at full blast! The maid, Mary, looked after Ena extremely well, and in fact paid her a visit at the Tower in 1986, when Ena was back at the Wurlitzer in concert after 40 years.

With minimum rehearsal, Ena opened at the Tower Ballroom in early February, and the second most famous tower in the world advertised, in addition to Bertram Mills' Elephant Sextette, the Cairoli Brothers and the Children's Ballet, 'Dancing

'I'll Play To You' – Sandy Macpherson with Florence at a Regal Bridlington Sunday concert in 1939.

The man who adored Florence; her second husband, Lou Morris.

to Richard Crean and the Tower Band – Ena Baga at the organ'. The West Lancashire Evening Gazette went to town with a headline 'FAMOUS WOMAN ORGANIST FOR THE TOWER', quoting her as saying that she found Blackpool 'the most cosmopolitan thing since I last saw Piccadilly and Shaftesbury Avenue' and the people 'as vital as one could wish'. In turn, they described Ena as a 'vivacious brunette, born within the sound of Bow Bells.' The Gazzette expressed the opinion that her ability would reassure her and give her confidence in succeeding an organist of the fame and calibre of Reginald Dixon. 'When she takes her place at the celebrated Wurlitzer on Monday night, it will mean the opening of a new phase of her career'. She told the reporter that the acoustic properties of the Ballroom were excellent, with no echo and no time-lag between the organ chambers (above the stage) and the console. 'But then, of course, in a place like Blackpool, where they do everything so well, they should be. I don't know Blackpool, but I've heard plenty about it.' She was able to get to know Blackpool well during the course of the next four years or so.

For her first broadcast at the BBC Theatre Organ in January 1938, Ena had opened with a selection of tunes associated with Harlem, for example, 'Harlem Nocturne' and simply 'Harlem', and, with an element of super-stition, she chose the same selection for her dance debut at the Tower. 'Call it superstition – call it anything you want, but I could not play anything else. After all, this selection heralded my success with the BBC. I decided that it might be a little nice herald for

42

A good-looking lady at a handsome console! Ena at the Regal Bridlington Compton, c1939.

my Blackpool contract.' She noted that there was geat vitality in the dancing at Blackpool, and the tempo was a shade faster. It suited her, and she was prepared to do anything to please the 'customers'.

She says she could sense a little prejudice when she first started, but this is hardly surprising when one considers the enormous popularity of her predecessor. When the Wurlitzer was first installed at the Tower, in 1929, it had not proved particularly popular and, when Reginald Dixon was appointed on a trial basis in 1930, he was told that he had to make a success of it or both he and the organ would go! The success he made of the Wurlitzer as an accompaniment to dancing is legendary, and his was a very difficult act to follow. Ena started by playing for seven days a week without a break, including dancing sessions in the morning for servicemen and women if it was wet and they couldn't do their square-bashing! There were also Sunday concerts, the first of which was on Easter Sunday, April 13th, with nearly 9,000 attending! A tremendous reception was given Ena at the Wurlitzer and Richard Crean with the Orchestra, while Webster Booth and Anne Ziegler, and Ivor Moreton and Dave Kay (Harry Roy's popular piano duettists) all had to give encores.

After several months' of this, Ena began to feel the pressure, and so she was given Sundays off and theatre organists from the services were engaged for the Sunday concerts. Able-Seaman Howlett came to do one of the first, and we guess one of the best! Taught by Quentin Maclean, John Howlett played for silent films at Bournemouth, London and Birmingham, opening the Regent Dudley in 1928. From there he went to Belfast, Preston, Stourbridge and Handsworth, opening the Luxor Eastbourne in 1933. He then spent five years with County Cinemas, before enlisting in the Royal Navy in 1941. After the war, he was at Wimbledon and Swiss Cottage, being appointed to the Odeon Flagship at Leicester Square in 1947, following the death of James Bell. Organist and composer, he was a particularly good broadcaster and his 'Moonlight Lullaby' programmes from Leicester Square will long be remembered.

A later Assistant Manager at the Leicester Square Odeon was Terence Dene, who had played at the Gaumont Chadwell Heath before and immediately after the war, and he obtained leave of absence from the RAF to do one of the Sunday shows. Two others were Watson Holmes and Frank Todd, and the Tower staff talked beforehand of the forthcoming appearance of 'Sherlock Holmes' and 'Sweeney Todd'. Ena says that she was told that Sidney Torch, who was based in Blackpool with the RAF, was up in one of the balconies one evening listening to her, but he did not present himself.

Ena's first broadcast from the Tower Wurlitzer went out on St. Patrick's Day, March 17th, and was the afternoon session of 'Music While You Work'. What must have been a very nice broadcast followed at lunch-time on March 28th, opening with Eric Coates' March-London Bridge (from his London Suite) followed by Quentin Maclean's delightful 'Parade of the Sunbeams', 'Orient Express', an RAF Medley, Friml's 'Love Everlasting', and concluding with a selection, 'Fifty Years of Song'. I should like to have heard it. Ena's popularity at the Tower was quickly established, and this, together with the broadcasts, brought her an enormous fan-mail. She received a proposal of marriage from an Irish doctor (photo enclosed); a widower with seven children wanted to discuss the International Situation with her (one wonders if it was his own situation he really wished to discuss!) one man 'used to think nothing of women as organists, but you have changed my opinion'; an RAF man wrote 'You are playing good enough for a man'; and another fan said 'Fancy a little thing like you making so much noise!'. Broadcasts continued regularly and usually ended with a 'Tower Request Medley' or 'Tower Popular Medley'.

'Popular Hit Medley' was the title of Ena's first recording made at the Tower in August 1941, issued on the Regal Zonophone label; in company with issues by Harry Roy and His Band, Dinah Shore, Black Dyke Mills Band, Harry Leader and His Band and Reginald Dixon. The 78rpm disc began with 'Sergeant Sally', 'There I Go' and 'Yes, My Darling Daughter', backed by 'A Little Steeple Pointing to a Star' and 'Waltzing in the Clouds'. It has remained a very popular record with organ enthusiasts, especially the marvellous jazzy rendering of 'Yes, My Darling Daughter', with its double-bass pedalling at the end. The Regal Zonophone leaflet carried a nice picture of Ena purporting to be at the Tower Blackpool organ. It wasn't. It was at the Compton at the Regal Bridlington. In the same month, the comedy trio from Radio's 'Happidrome', Mr. Lovejoy, Enoch and Ramsbottom, recorded at the Grand Theatre and there were two records from Anne Zeigler and Webster Booth, all appearing in Blackpool. 'Musica' of the Blackpool Gazette & Herald commented on the prominence of Blackpool artists on current recordings, making particular note of Ena's record.

In September, 'Musica' also coined the title 'Queen of the Keyboard' in an article about Ena's popularity at Blackpool. 'Her versatility is demonstrated during her recitals at the Sunday concerts in the Tower Ballroom, where she is partnered by Roy Page, another clever organist, and her recent recording of an original arrangement of popular 'hits' has brought her many well-deserved congratulations.' On September 16th, 'Children's Hour', the loss of which is much lamented, took listeners to Blackpool in 'I Do Like to be Beside the Seaside'. One was invited to meet Mr. Lovejoy, Enoch and Ramsbottom, hear the opening of the Happi-drome show (from the Grand Theatre); visit the Tower Circus; and 'listen to a well-known theatre organist . . .' Why Radio Times could not have stated which I don't know, unless they thought it might give away the location!

Three 'Grand All Star Concerts' were given on September 21st; at the New Opera House were Webster Booth & Anne Zeigler, Frank Randle and Teddy Brown (the famous and mighty xylophonist); at the Grand Theatre Leslie ('Hutch') Hutchinson and Hal Swain; and at the Tower Ballroom Ena Baga and Florence de Jong (at the 'Wonder Wurlitzer') with Beatrice Baga, violiniste. Admission to the Tower to hear the Ladies was 1/2d, including tax! Immediately after this, Ena had to go into the Victoria Hospital for a major operation (the removal of an ovarian cyst) and was unable to return to the Tower for nearly three months. Her place at the Wurlitzer was taken by Florence, who interrupted a series of charity concerts to do so. Ena felt that she could never fully express her gratitude to the doctors and nurses at Blackpool's Victoria Hospital, and, back on the air on December 12th, she selected music to relate to the host of letters she received in hospital.

Florence returned to her series of 'Celebrity Organ Recitals' – in the Rhondda

45

Show a leg there! The girls relax in the sun at Southend. Left to right: Beatrice, Celeste, Florence and Ena.

Valley. From December 1941 to May 1944, she appeared at the Saron Chapel Ynishir, Tonpandy Central Hall, Bethania Chapel Treorchy (with the Treorchy Royal Welsh Male Choir), Salem Chapel Llwynypia, and in concert at the Capitol Cardiff ('at the theatre organ' but this was a Hammond Lafleur electronic in a small box to the left of the stage). At the same time, Florence was playing at her husband's theatres and broadcasting.

Back at the Tower, Ena was again presenting Sunday afternoon and evening shows, in which she included short feature spots by men and women of the services stationed in the North-West of England. One morning, a little boy called Eric presented himself at Ena's office and asked for an audition at the Wurlitzer! Only 14, the organ dwarfed but did not intimidate him, and, as a result of his 20-minute tuition with Ena, he appeared in the spotlight in one of her Sunday shows. 'He was as composed and efficient as if he had been playing for years', said Ena. One wonders what became of him and if he took up music as a profession?

A letter was received from a young lady, written in an authoritative manner and asking for an audition for a Sunday appearance. The lady claimed to have sung to munition workers and to the Forces no less than 160 times, and called herself 'The Pocket Vesta'. She added that she was 'nearly 13'. The young lady duly appeared in a Sunday concert and was a great success, her repertoire including one of Stanley Holloway's well-known monologues. The one about the family visiting Blackpool and Young Albert being eaten by a lion, perhaps? 'And him in his Sunday clothes too!'. 'Confidence", says Ena. 'I was astonished. Thirteen would at one time have meant 'do-ray-me'. Now, it's Vo-do-de-oh!.'

Like Florence in South Wales, Ena appeared for charity at special Sunday concerts in different parts of the country. On February 1st, 1942, she was the top of the bill in a 'Grand Organ Recital & Concert' in aid of Mrs. Winston Churchill's Russian Red Cross Appeal at the Majestic Cinema Darlington (later Odeon). The organ at the Majestic was a Compton of 8 ranks, opened in 1932 by Frank Matthew, who had assisted at the New Gallery from 1925 to 1926, going on to open similar Wurlitzers for PCT at the Havelock Sunderland, the Regent Bristol, and becoming resident at the Granada Walthamstow in 1931. Harry Millen took over from Frank Matthew at Darlington, assuming the role of Manager/Organist by 1939. It was a well-publicised event when Darlington presented such a famous star at their one an only theatre organ! Ena was supported by seven variety acts, including BBC tenor R. Hawdon Gibson.

On Monday, September 21st 1942, Ena gave her 50th broadcast, taking part, with Molly Forbes and vocalist Esther Coleman, in 'Sandy's Half-Hour', this being the second programme in which the evening was entirely devoted to ladies. During the course of a short interview with Sandy, Ena accidentally gave herself another sister! Sandy: 'If I remember rightly, Ena, you have musical sisters. And wasn't your father a composer as well?' Ena: 'Yes, Sandy, he was. Three of my sisters are organists and one a violinist.' Keen-eared listeners wrote to her, saying that the well-known Baga family was larger than they thought!

However, a short time afterwards, sadly there was one less. On December 9th, 1942, 'Papa' Constantine Baga died at the family home in Southchurch Avenue, Southend, aged 78. He had been ill for four weeks. Two of his best-known compositions were 'Passing Thoughts', written for Florence as a signature tune when she first went to the New Gallery, and 'Tender Heart'. The latter was broadcast in his honour by Ena on the following January 6th, a last request being that she should play it for him. There was also a memorial service at the Sacred Heart Church, where Constantine had been Choirmaster 30 years before and Ena the young organist.

On a much happier note, Ena went back to church to play for the wedding of her friend Jane Taylor, who became Mrs. G.C. Collyer at St. John's Parish Church, Blackpool.

In 1943 Tower Ballroom dancers had the pace and tempo set by Vic Filmer, who was currently conducting the Tower Band, with, of course, Ena at the Wurlitzer. On Easter Sunday, for the bargain admission price of 1/6, there were afternoon and evening concerts featuring Reginald Dixon, on leave from the RAF, and Ena Baga. What an experience that must have been!

During the war, Blackpool was one of the busiest towns in England and certainly the busiest seaside resort. More than 1,700 civil servants were housed in Blackpool's largest hotels, mainly from the Ministry of Pensions, and the Ministry of Food were occupying the Fernley Hotel. 'RAF Station Blackpool' had 45,000 airmen billeted throughout the town, and nearly 800,000 recruits were given their reception training at Blackpool, drilling and square-bashing in the main being carried out on the Promenade and sands. The Headquarters of RAF operations was the Winter Garden complex, training films being shown in the large and magnificent Opera House, while the Empress Ballroom was in use as a gymnasium! What that would have done to the beautiful sprung floor, I can only guess! At the beginning of the war, nearly 40,000 evacuees were transported to the town, and there were further large contingents in 1940 from Liverpool and Manchester, and from South London when the V1 flying-bomb campaign started in June 1944. All these people, together with the usual visitors, required entertainment in the evenings and at week-ends, and Ena and her colleagues were kept more than busy.

There were RAF stations at Kirkham and Weeton and an American Air Force base at Warton, near Lytham, whereas many Polish Air Force personnel were also stationed near the town. Polish National Day took place in 1944 on the 153rd Anniversary of the first Polish Constitution, and to commemorate this, a musical programme was given at the Jubilee Theatre, consisting of national songs and dances by members of Revoe School (in Polish costume) and Ena, a member of the 'Polish Hearth', playing Chopin, Paderewski and Richard Adinsell's 'Warsaw Concerto', from 'Dangerous Moonlight'; a piece she was later to record with Florence at the organ for the BBC, at the New Gallery.

Mention of Florence, reminds me that she was featured in 'Woman's Illustrated' in October 1944, in Godfrey Winn's 'Scrapbook of the War'. Writing from a hotel by the Helford River, near Helston in Cornwall, Godfery Winn mingles with the guests in a small ante-room to the dining room for an old-fashioned sing-song. 'And then the music changes into 'Passing Thoughts', the signature tune of the guest artist at the piano, whom you have heard so many times over the wireless and in public concerts. Florence is my favourite guest in the hotel; not only is she good to look at with her find dark eyes and golden skin but she is good to be with, because she radiates warmth and genuine feeling and a reassuring sense of harmony. And she achieves this not only through her playing, but also through her technique in living. She has learnt the greatest secret of success in life – no matter what the circumstances or the company, be yourself. Yes, it is FLORENCE DE JONG.' A combination of Italian descent and the Astral sign of Leo?

In addition to hosts of civil servants, RAF personnel and evacuees, many distinguished and important people were in Blackpool, including the Buyers for Marks & Spencer's. Ena became friendly with Mr. and Mrs. Ernest Michaels, who had taken a furnished house in Devonshire Road, overlooking the golf-course. Ena played golf with Ernest Michaels, and became a highly proficient player. In April 1945 she was presented with three golfing trophies at the North Shore Ladies' Golf Club, 'the Lady de Frece Trophy', the 'Dunderdale Silver Trophy' and the 'Parkinson Cup'; the first time all three trophies had been won by one member. Professional artists and agents were in Blackpool, and Ena would often visit the office of Lawrence Wright, running through new publications on the piano for him. She met Leslie ('Hutch') Hutchinson there, and one morning when Richard Tauber came bounding up the stairs, she struck up 'You Are My Heart's Delight'. On entering, Tauber exclaimed with great delight 'Ah, it is in the right key!'. Richard Tauber could be found every morning in the Oyster Bar under Blackpool Tower. 'Hutch' was serenaded in Lawrence Wright's office with a few bars of 'These Foolish Things', for which of course he was well-known. Lawrence Wright remarked that none of the other organists could play the piano like Ena.

The Polish Officers billeted in Blackpool were expert bridge players, and Ena learned bridge at the golf club. She has enjoyed bridge ever since.

After the death of 'Papa', 'Mama Baga' would come and stay at Blackpool and, during Ena's afternoon session, would sit in a shelter on the Promenade. On her first visit, when Ena went to collect her, she said 'What language do they speak in this town? I can't understand it'. Not the first person to be confused by West Lancashire dialect!

With all the activity going on in the town, it is amazing that only 8 people were killed and 14 injured during the war, but things might have been very different if a bomb that fell on the Central Station one afternoon had landed a little further north! The Ballroom was crowded at the time but the only disturbance was a dull thud. Another bomb dropped on the golf course, and it seems that someone over the other side must have known that Ena was in Blackpool, boosting the morale of the populace.

Two other famous people Ena met were Ivor Novello and his mother, Madame Novello Davies, both of whom stayed at the Huntsman. A nervous dance-band vocalist due to give an audition with Mme Novello Davies asked Ena to accompany her to help give her confidence. Mme. Davies remarked 'My dear, I wonder if you realise how lucky you are to have such a good accompanist?'.

During the winter seasons at Blackpool, Ena's appearances were confined to relieving the Band and two Sunday concerts. She also relieved Elton Roberts and Roy Page at the Empress Ballroom Wurlitzer. One evening a teacher of dancing introduced himself, and, at her request, checked Ena's tempos. He said that they were good, commenting only that the quicksteps were a shade too fast (but, remember that Blackpool dancers liked their Ballroom Dances a little faster), and that her slow waltzes needed to be a little quicker. The long established 'Children's Ballet' was presented at the Tower by Annette Schultz, accompanied by Ena at the Wurlitzer. There were two performances in the afternoon, and Ena then stood by to play during the band interval at 8 p.m. Before her Sunday off was granted, she would also perform two Sunday concerts. Oh, and she would also play a morning dance session if it was wet, which it often was!

'Top O' Th' Tower', a prewar annual event, returned to the air on Saturday August 18th, 1945, with front-page billing in 'Radio Times'. Listeners to The Light Programme, which had replaced the 'Forces', heard Vera Lynn at the Palace Theatre; George Black's 'Hip, Hip, Horray' from the Opera House with Tessie O'Shea, Jewell & Warriss and Felix Mendelssohn's Hawaiian Serenaders; and Flt.Lt. Reginald Dixon and Ena Baga at the organ of the Tower Ballroom. One of the last broadcasts by Ena from the Tower was on Sunday September 30th, when 'Sunday Half-Hour' came from the Ballroom. Community Hymn-singing was led by the Blackpool Glee and Madrigal Society, accompanied by Ena and introduced by Reginald Dixon. Mrs. Todd, of Sherwood Nottingham, wrote 'I would like to tell you how we here in Nottingham enjoyed the community singing broadcast from the Tower Ballroom on Sunday evening. As we listened and joined in the old familiar hymns, I could visualise the scene – the choir – and Miss Baga at the organ – and one thought of friends away and of voices

The Regal Bridlington; architect C. Edmond Wilford, ARIBA (photo: John Maltby).

now stilled. I hope that other friends away listened and enjoyed it as we did.'

In December, 1945, Reginald Dixon returned to civilian life and the Tower, where he was to remain until retirement on Easter Sunday, 1970. Ena was asked if she would like to stay as Reg's assistant but she declined, preferring to return to London. A send-off in the form of a joint Sunday afternoon concert was arranged and, knowing her fondness for vegetables, the Tower Management gave her an enormous basket of them, designed like a Harvest Festival. And so Ena bade farewell to a crowded ballroom, after nearly five years as the Tower Organist. On the day, 'Seasider' of the Evening Gazette reported: 'Famous signature tune, 'Smoke Gets In Your Eyes' will make Tower organist, vivacious brunette Ena Baga, a little moist-eyed when she plays it on Saturday night. In her room behind the Tower stage, packed with photographs of celebrities and hundreds of tributes from Forces members, she recalled the war years, packed with heart-warming memories, broadcasts, recordings, concerts, innumerable friendships.'

One tangible memory is a clock in white enamel, gilt and polished wood, representing the Tower Ballroom stage proscenium. The clock is the work of T. Hume and J. Tarrant, two craftsmen, who made the gift as a token of happy moments at the Tower with Ena.

CHAPTER SEVEN

Ena's return to London co-incided with husband Jim's demob from the RAF, and they went to live with Jim's mother in a bungalow at Shepperton-on-Thames. Her first appearance, or re-appearance, in the South was for a week commencing on Christmas Eve at the Ritz Tunbridge Wells. The Ritz was the first cinema to be actually built by Union Cinemas, although they had taken over many others. The organ, a seven-rank Compton with the Compton patent Solo Cello (an amplified mechanical 'cello, which I always think sounds like a cow with stomach-ache), was opened by Alex Taylor in 1934 and visited by members of the Union team, including Lloyd Thomas, Neville Meale, Harold Ramsay (Musical Director), Rudy Lewis, Phil Park, Robinson Cleaver, Sidney Torch, and Cornish Wonder Boy Organist Dudley Savage, until the collapse of Union at the end of 1937. The Ritz was one of a handful of theatres that did not pass to ABC with the Union circuit, and relied on visiting guest organists.

Next, a couple of weeks with Betty Hutton, Humphrey Bogart and Gary Cooper at the Empress Hackney, playing a small 5-rank Compton, and a few weeks with Gaumont-British, at the Regent Brighton, Trocadero Elephant & Castle (Rudy Lewis was visiting the Regal Edmonton), Gaumont Peckham and the New Cross Kinema. In between the GB engagements, Ena did a special two-weeks from March 11th 1946 at the Century Clacton-on-Sea, playing a seven-rank Christie with a unique and attractive illuminated surround. The name 'Christie' is taken from John Christie, the Chairman of Hill, Norman & Beard, organ builders, who started building unit (theatre) organs in 1926. John Christie went on to found Glyndebourne Opera, first at the Tunbridge Wells Opera House and then at the purpose-built Opera House at his country seat of Glyndebourne. A glorious eccentric, it was said that he used to wear white tie and tails for the evening opera with sandals which he removed to paddle in the lily-pond on hot nights!

Broadcasts continued, from GB theatres such as the Trocadero Elephant & Castle (on the largest Wurlitzer in Europe), the Gaumont-State Kilburn, Gaumont Camden Town (an old friend), and at the BBC Theatre Organ, a 27-rank Moller organ with 5 keyboards, originally built for Reginald Foort to tour the music halls.

After a year's absence from Blackpool, Ena returned at the beginning of December 1946 for a month's engagement at the Odeon, where Florence had made a guest appearance a few weeks before. The organ at the Blackpool Odeon was a Conacher, originally installed in Ena's second home, Southend, and opened there at the County Cinemas' Ritz by Quentin Maclean in 1935. James Swift and Douglas Reeve made guest appearances, and residents from 1935 to 1938 were Andrew Fenner and Guy Hindell, the latter doubling with the Astoria in the same town. The 12-rank organ with 'phantom' grand piano was transferred to the Odeon Blackpool in 1946 and re-opened there by Al Bollington from the Paramount/Odeon Tottenham Court Road. Jess Yates and Tommy Nicholson were both resident, and the last guest organist was Bobby Pagan who took part in

Miss Blackpool 1941-1945! Ena succeeds Reginald Dixon at the Tower Ballroom, Blackpool, where she soon became very popular.

A sister to assist her! Florence deputises for Ena at the Blackpool Tower Wurlitzer during the latter's spell in hospital.

two broadcasts featuring all 5 organs in Blackpool: the Tower, Empress, Opera House, Palace Ballroom and Odeon. A Blackpool lady wrote to the press that she was looking forward to Ena's return, and said that she knew of a soldier who had quarreled with his girl friend before going out East, but Ena Baga's music and letters were the means of re-uniting them. Such is the power of music and personality!

In July, 1947, Ena returned to Bournemouth for three guest weeks at the GB-Regent, playing a beautiful little Wurlitzer of 9 ranks, similar to that at the Regent Brighton. This organ was heard regularly on the air in the late forties and early fifties in a series 'Melody For Late Evening" with Ronald Brickell, a vocalist, and violinist Harold C. Gee, leader of the orchestra at Bournemouth's Bath Hotel, a place much visited by Florence and Ena in later years. While in Bournemouth, Ena assisted the Gaumont-British film star Dermot Walsh to judge the Holiday Queen of Bournemouth at the Town Hall. The 'Queen" also received a sash on the stage of the Regent, while the Keyboard Queen provided suitable music at the Wurlitzer.

'Leading Lady' is a title that could well apply to Ena, and 'Leading Lady' is also the title of a novel by D.L. Murray, set in Blackpool and published by Hodder & Stoughton in November 1947. About people of the theatre, it is written by someone who knows the theatre and knows Blackpool '. . . now arose a loud outburst of applause as Ena Baga in the majesty of her long white and gold gown appeared

52

Room for a few inside! A crowded Tower Ballroom in 1942, with Ena standing beside the Wurlitzer console.

upon the stage and mounted the console of the great Wurlitzer organ. Enthroned there in an aureole of tinted lights, high above the heads of the people, she might have been the priestess of some colossal temple. With delicate fingering she sent out the soft waves of her signature tune, subduing the mighty instrument to a tone of reverie. Then, as she opened to a full-mouthed diapason, the elated worshippers streamed forth upon the floor, blending the swish of hundreds of feet with the rhythmical swell and throb that poured through the vast hall . . .' Ena's copy of the book is dedicated 'To Ena, who gave me some of my happiest memories of Blackpool by her art and her friendship, with the affectionate good wishes of David Murray.'

Early in 1948, Ena returned again to Blackpool for a couple of guest weeks at the Odeon. The console surround of the Conacher was unique and resembled butterfly wings. It must have looked terrific when illuminated. Unfortunately, when the organ was removed from the Odeon between 1966 and 1968 the orchestra pit had been covered and it was not possible to get the beautiful surround out.

Towards the end of May, Ena was invited to Copenhagen for a three-week guest engagement at the Palladium, which had a Wurlitzer with an unusual console, eliptical-shaped, and which arose back to the audience, swivelling the organist into view as it came up! The Danish theatre organist Mogens Kilde and Bobby Pagan, who had already visited, contacted Ena about the trip, and she went with Chris Morris, a golfing pal, sailing on the 'Crown Prince Frederick'. Not long after they

Ena receiving the THREE golfing cups she won in one year at Blackpool. (photo: Blackpool Gazette and Herald Ltd).

left England, they were drooling at the mouth at the sight of the Smogsbrod laid out in the ship's dining room, but there would be plenty of opportunity for that! They disembarked at Esbjerg and took a train to Copenhagen, where they were met by the Secretary of the Palladium Cinema, who spoke no English! This was particularly unfortunate, as Ena discovered that, instead of her own, she had brought her husband's passport and there were lengthy explanations. Her friend Chris saw the funny side of the situation, and broke into an appropriate verse of 'Among My Souvenirs'.

The Palladium was a very friendly cinema, with a magnificent bar in the foyer and a special 'nursery' for children and dogs. Ena was introduced to the Inspector (equivalent of Manager) and given a large gin and Italian, whereas she was really dying for a cup of tea! They were taken to a hotel in a square near the Palladium, which was adjacent to the famous Tivoli Gardens. Ena felt that the theatre management did not know quite what to expect from their first visiting lady organist from England, but they were very helpful and hospitable and the rehearsal next morning went off well. Everywhere they went, a Union Flag appeared on their table, and they were invited to various Danish homes to eat. In the flats, Ena noticed that, instead of curtains, there were trailing plants all around the windows, and the tables were invariably groaning with food and drink. After one of these receptions, the organ console felt as if it were rising at an angle of 45 degrees! Schnapps on ice with an enormous meal at 10 in the morning is not perhaps the most suitable prelude to opening a show at 12.30p.m.!

Southend to Blackpool! The Conacher theatre organ installed in the Odeon Blackpool in 1946 came from the Ritz Southend-on-Sea, as did Ena who returned to Blackpool in 1946 by popular demand to play it.

Celeste was twice resident at Garon's Cinema, Southend, playing an early Christie theatre organ of 1927. Here she is in 1950.

Broadway, Sheerness, in the forties showing the Argosy, Hippodrome and Rio cinemas, all owned at that time by Lou Morris. The fourth operating cinema, the Ritz, around the corner in Wood Street, was built and run by Lou, giving him a monopoly in Sheerness. All four were sold to the Essoldo circuit in 1947.

Ena and Chris were taken on many outings, visiting castles and the seaside at Klampenborg, where, in a side show, they saw Lilian Harvey, star of 'Congress Dances', remembered by Ena from her days at the Tivoli. They also went to 'Charley's Bar', kept by an Englishman in King's New Town, and to the Tuborg Brewery, where Ena queried why the bottles were clamped in a wooden frame. 'We like to see how it travels' was the reply. She was invited back to the Brewery to an all-night party on the evening before she left Denmark, when their hostess smoked a pipe and everyone had to dress as cowboys. Ena played the piano, and they danced the night away! The 'Inspector' at the Palladium also did not speak English, but he literally cried when Ena left, begging her to 'stay, stay!' (the one word he knew). While at the Palladium, Ena broadcast two or three times and even managed a greeting in Danish. The boat for the return was the 'Parkstone', and the North Sea was at its very worst. Inveterate traveller that she was, friend Chris looked a little green and they both got soaked when the decks were washed down! Ena vowed that future trips would be by air!

At the end of the war, eldest sister Celeste had finished touring with Beatrice and returned to Southend, playing at the Gliderdrome Dance Hall and Skating Rink. In 1947, she took up the post of organist at Garon's Cinema, where Ena had played piano for silent films but where a 7-rank Christie theatre organ had been installed in 1927. Sister Florence had travelled further than any of them, on account of a new business venture by husband Lou Morris.

By 1946, Lou Morris had disposed of a dozen of his cinemas: Capitol Wembley to Medway Cinemas; Cosy Harrow and Regal Loftus to independent operators; Playhouse Dewsbury, Princess Dagenham, Plaza Worthing, Majestic Bridgnorth, Regals at Bridlington & Walton to ABC; Astoria Chesham to Shipman & King; Carlton Norwich to Odeon and Plaza Sutton to Granada. He had retained the Savoy Willesden and Astoria Boscombe, also acquiring the Picture House Chelsea (renamed Ritz), Palace Bridgnorth, Savoy Boscombe, Cameo & Plaza Margate, and the Argosy, Hippodrome & Rio Sheerness, the latter from Gaumont-British. At that time he was also Chairman of Twentieth-Century Cinemas, controlling the Century Clacton and the Empress Hackney, both theatres visited by Ena as guest organist.

Lou entered into a contract with General Jan Christiaan Smuts, Prime Minister of the Union of South Africa, to build houses for the natives at a factory in Germinston, near Durban, in partnership with a man named Mulberry, famous for the prefabricated harbour towed across the English Channel in 1944 and erected off the Normandy beaches during the invasion of Europe by Allied Forces. So, Lou and Florence went out to South Africa in 1947, staying in Durban. The Natal Mercury carried a picture of Florence talking to Tommy McLennan at a special party given in her honour. Tommy M cLennan was resident at a Wurlitzer in the Metro Theatre Durban, and Florence was asked to deputise for him while on holiday. General Smuts' premiership ended in 1948 (he died in 1950), and most

Florence also appeared as guest organist at the 3,000-seater Blackpool Odeon, although she later said she never did!

Florence as guest organist at the Metro Theatre Wurlitzer, Durban, in 1950 (photo: Keith Adams, Durban).

Lou and Florence living it up in South Africa around 1948 (photo: Happy Snaps, Beach, Durban.

unfortunately his successor placed an embargo on the import of raw materials, which meant that Lou and his partner could not continue with the house-building. A considerable amount of capital was lost in this abortive venture and, returning to England in a very distressed state, Lou sustained a stroke. The doctor advised Florence that Lou should be removed from the strain of London life, and they bought a beautiful flat at Black Rock, Brighton, overlooking the sea.

Two others in the cinema business who emigrated to South Africa were Albert and Sid O'Connor, who owned AOC Theatres, including the Regal Kennington in South East London. The Regal was a very modern, well-designed theatre with 2,000 seats, opened in 1938 with one of the comparatively few electronic organs in a cinema – a Hammond Lafleur. It differed from the one installed for Lou Morris at Grays in that it had a full-size illuminated surround of the 'Rainbow' variety and looked, to all intents and purposes, like a theatre pipe organ. Only the sound was different! Ena appeared as guest organist in April and August, 1948, and the South London Press made a splash of her second visit, reporting on her experiences in Copenhagen. By the beginning of August, when she paid her second visit, the Regal had been sold to Granada, and the press advertisement for Alice Faye & Jack Oakie in 'The Great American Broadcast,' and Fred Astaire & Rita Hayworth in 'You Were Never Lovelier' announced the Regal as 'The Service-With-A-Smile Theatre' and the large figure of 'Sergeant G' was proudly covering the top corner. Guest Organist Ena Baga presented 'Holiday Sing-Song'.

'She's scintillating . . . gay . . . and is Guest Organist October 4 week at Granada Harrow', said a card hand-out, with a very nice photograph of Ena at the Tower Ballroom console. Granada were always tops at publicity. For example, the arrival of Harold Ramsay at the Granada Tooting in 1932 was heralded weeks before with large posters, saying 'Who is Mr. X?' and whenever a theatre was taken over, the bill-boards for weeks before would state 'Start saying GRANADA. Please pronounce it 'Grah-nah-dah'. A similar publicity card was produced for Ena's appearance at the Granada Kingston-on-Thames, the week before Harrow.

CHAPTER EIGHT

Towards the end of 1948, Ena received a 'phone call from Neil Salmon of J. Lyons & Co., saying that electric organs were all the rage in caféterias in the United States, and Lyons were about to introduce their first Caféteria at the Oxford Corner House, Tottenham Court Road. (It doesn't now seem possible that caféterias, i.e. self-service, were not around in the UK until after the Second World War). A Hammond had been installed in the new caféteria, on hire, and Neil Salmon wished Ena Baga to go and play it. As this was regular employment, rather than free-lance guesting that could be spasmodic, Ena accepted. A superb meal could be had at the ground floor Caféteria for 1/-, and the new-style eaterie became very popular. Ena sat upon a dais at one end with the Model B Hammond and a grand piano, so placed that she could turn from one to the other.

The Manager's name at the Oxford Corner House was Mr. Shepherd, and, watching all the people around her munching and chewing, Ena loved to play 'Sheep May Safely Graze'. There was some initial picketing from the orchestral musicians who were used to having the monopoly in restaurants but Ena weathered the storm and settled down to a new phase in her musical career. Self-service was introduced at the Corner Houses at Coventry Street, Marble Arch and the Strand, with at least six organs. Ena had heard that Compton, who had pioneered the electrone with the Melotone Unit in 1935, followed by the 'Theatrone', a complete electronic organ on the same principle, were about to introduce a new model, called the 'Melotone'. Thinking it right to promote a British organ, she asked the M.D. for Joe Lyons, Mr. Moss, to meet J.I. Taylor, the Principal Demonstrator, at the Compton works at Acton. Leslie Spurling met them and Ena explained that she thought this a golden opportunity to promote the new Compton electronic organ – in London. Compton had not decided whether to hire the new models out or not, so, realising that it would be a waste of time, the Model B Hammonds were hired from Boosey & Hawkes instead. Eventually, the hired Hammonds were all replaced by Compton Melotones, bought new from Acton. I can remember the sad look on Ray Baines' face at the Strand on the last night with the Hammond, 'It's like saying good-bye to an old friend', he said.

Opposite the Oxford Corner House was, and still is, the Dominion Theatre. Designed by W. & T.R. Millburn, it was built in 1929 on the site of a Fun Fair, previously occupied by Meux' Brewery until 1922. The Dominion opened with a golfing musical that only ran for 148 performances, followed by another short-lived musical and variety with Maurice Chevalier. Films were then tried, interspersed with live shows, but after Richard Tauber starred in 'A Land of Smiles' in 1932, Gaumont-British acquired it for their 'Flagship' and films reigned supreme. A 14-rank Compton was opened by Fredric Bayco in 1933, followed by Felton Rapley, Tommy Dando, Felton Rapley again and Charles Smitton. A young organist arrived from Wolverhampton, via Finchley, in 1950 and his name was William Davies, later to achieve fame with the BBC as pianist, organist,

Dame Anna Neagle visits the Cinema and Television Benevolent Fund residential home at Glebelands, Wokingham. Glebelands benefactor, Lou Morris, is to the left but one of Dame Anna. (photo: Press and Weekly News).

conductor and arranger for such programmes as 'Melodies for You', 'Just William' and 'Friday Night is Music Night'. Bill Davies often went into the Corner House for a bite to eat, and he and Ena became god friends, as he recalled years later at Gunton Hall for Ena's 'This Is My Life'.

After just over three years at the Corner House, Ena went to see Neil Salmon to tell him that it was her husbands dearest wish to run a Public House, and they had decided to take the tenancy of The Jolly Blacksmith at Fulwell, Middlesex. Neil Salmon's reaction to this news was – 'When you come to your senses, ring me up!' The Jolly Blacksmith was very close to Fulwell Golf Course, and, although they could occasionally play golf, they had no life together to speak of. It is no secret that running a public house is very hard work, very often for little reward. At Fulwell there were five tills that had to be added up every night, and, Ena says, if they made a little profit, up went the rent! Ena built up the business by playing in the Lounge, on piano and Clavioline (an electronic keyboard, featured also by John Howlett at the Odeon Leicester Square, by John Madin on the Granada circuit, and by Sandy Macpherson, who replaced the fifth manual of the BBC Möller in the Jubilee Chapel with a Clavioline for some months). Sister Beatrice would occasionally visit, and she and Ena would perform duets in the Lounge. Sandy Macpherson, with his faithful Secretary Joyce Heppell, went to see Ena several times, and, true to the blood of his ancestors, partook of a few scotches.

In 1953, Ralph Bartlett, General Secretary of the Theatre Organ Club, arranged a Sunday afternoon visit to the pub, and the members were entertained on a very hot afternoon, with much waving of Ena's Japanese fan in between numbers. At last, we met, and I shyly asked her if I could have a signed photograph, preferably the nice one in 'Theatre Organ World' taken at the Regal Bridlington. Ena obliged, and told me to bend my back to form a writing desk. I was struck with her strong and friendly personality, to the extent that we were on Christian-name terms before the day was out. A slightly jealous Ralph was heard to remark: 'You all start the day callin' her 'Mrs Brown' an' finish up callin' 'er Ena!'

Meanwhile, Florence and Lou Morris were still in their lovely flat at Brighton, and, in 1949, Florence made some guest appearances, at the Regal Guernsey in June, which, at that time, still belonged to Lou. In 1946, Lou had extended his activities in the Channel Islands, opening, for example, a cinema in Alderney in an Old Presbyterian Church and known as the Lyceum. In 1950 the Trocadero Elephant & Castle was presenting a season of 'Sunday Evening at the Troc' variety shows, and in February, with 'Professor' Jimmy Edwards and The Sky Masters dance orchestra topping the bill, the prelude was performed at the organ by Florence de Jong.

Early in October, 1954, Lou and Florence stayed at the Dorchester Hotel and attended a Ladies' Night at the Anima Lodge. After the banquet Lou was taken ill with suspected food-poisoning, and was confined to bed at the Dorchester with Florence caring for him. Three days later, on October 11th, Lou died from a second stroke, at the age of 65. The funeral took place at Willesden Jewish Cemetry with 150 mourners, and a large number of relations, personal friends and acquaintances from the trade paid tribute to 'an old and valued friend'. Both the 'Kinematograph Weekly' and 'To-days Cinema' carried obituaries, the latter paying tribute to his keen interest in the Cinematograph Trade Benevolent Fund and the home for those retired from the business at Glebelands, Wokingham. Christmas, 1954, was a sad time for Florence, but she spent it with Ena and Jim at The Jolly Blacksmith and was not alone.

At the time of going to South Africa, Lou had sold the remainder of his cinemas; those at Sheerness and those of the Twentieth Century Cinemas, which he had created with S.H. Marshall (MP), J.P. Shaw and C.J. Willcox, being taken over by the expanding Essoldo circuit of Soly Sheckman. He had kept only the Classic Chelsea and one more recently acquired, the Ritz Stockwell. As was his wish, Florence carried on with Lou's business, including the operation of the two cinemas. The Daily Film Renter commented: 'Everybody without exception will be glad to know that Florence Morris is to keep going the cinema interests of her late husband, Lou. She will thus be keeping green the memory of one of the trade's best liked and most respected figures, and at the same time maintaining her own association with those very many people she can count among her friends.'

In 1956, Florence endowed a bed in the name of Lou at Glebelands, the Convalescent and Rest Home. She was a frequent visitor, and one week in January 1956 went with Ena and Beatrice to give the residents and convalescents a musical evening and to distribute chocolates.

Chocolates reminds me of children. During her five years at The Jolly Blacksmith, Ena played the little Compton theatre organ regularly for the

Three good fairies on the Glebelands Christmas Tree! Beatrice, Florence and Ena entertain the residents at the C.T.B.F. Home.

Saturday morning Children's Matinee at the nearby Odeon Twickenham. Opened in 1929 as the Luxor by Walter Bentley, the cinema was soon acquired by local entrepreneur Joseph Mears. His circuit was acquired by Odeon in 1944.

Towards the end of May, 1956, there were 400 children in the Odeon one Saturday morning waiting for the show to start when the stage curtains caught fire. Fortunately, the attendants immediately opened the five exit doors and the children left quietly and without any panic. The incident was fully reported on the local press: 'The organist, Miss Ena Baga, had just finished playing her signature tune, "Smoke Gets In Your Eyes", when the curtains began smoulding and then burst into flames. The flames shot up to the proscenium arch . . . Trying to keep the children calm, she switched to the theme song of "Robin Hood" and asked them to sing . . . They behaved perfectly and filed out . . . Miss Baga played the children out of the cinema with some lively tunes.' All in a day's work for a theatre organist. The Thames Valley Times added: 'The last word came from Ena Baga: "The smoke really got in my eyes that time".'

The following Saturday, Twickenham's new lady Mayor visited the Odeon and told the children that she was proud of the way they had responded to the instructions of the Manager and staff, for whom she called for three cheers, plus a very special one for Miss Baga.

Co-incidentally, another lady organist entered into the licensed trade, and this was Molly Forbes, who you may remember deputised for both Florence and Ena in 1937 and then took over from Ena at the Tivoli. At the end of her residency at the

Jolly Good Company at the Jolly Blacksmith! Beatrice and violin make a guest appearance at Ena and Jim's pub. Note the picture of Ena at Bridlington, and attached to the piano, a Clavioline - one of the first electronic keyboards

Warner Leicester Square, when Phil Finch returned from H.M. Forces in 1946, Molly joined ABC, first at the Regal Kingston-on-Thames, following Harold Coombs, who had succeeded the well-known Percy Whitlock as Borough Organist for Bournemouth at the Pavilion Theatre. Molly moved to the Regal Putney in 1947, which became her base theatre, and then to the Majestic Mitcham. She left ABC in 1956, and, after two seasons at the Davis' Theatre Croydon, and a short spell of free-lancing, Molly and her husband, Tony Holliday, took the 'Crown & Thistle' at Great Chesterford, on the borders of Essex and Cambridge. Like Ena, Molly popularised the inn and built up the business, her nightly playing in the Lounge Bar bringing customers from as far as Cambridge itself. Her husband did not like her singing at the organ, but encouraged by the clientele and fortified by a couple of gins, Molly would sometimes oblige.

It's not recorded whether Ena ever sang at her Hammond, but she certainly played the accordion and, in duet with Beatrice on violin, many very merry evenings must have been had at the 'Jolly Blacksmith'. However life in a pub is not all beer and skittles, and Ena found that she and her husband were almost living separate lives. She was never able to go out with him, as someone had to oversee the pub, which they decided was not the right one for them anyway. There were other difficulties and differences. For instance, Jim wanted a family but as a result of the operation at Blackpool Ena was unable to. In the end, the differences multiplied against the background of almost living apart, and they decided they should part. Jim took another pub in Kent, and Ena had an exciting offer to go to South Africa.

Florence at the Odeon, Blackpool c1948.

CHAPTER NINE

In 1948, the O'Connor Brothers, Albert & Sid, had sold their cinema interests, AOC Theatres, and emigrated to South Africa, investing in hotels. Florence had told Ena that the O'Connors were about to buy the Palm Beach Hotel at Margate, Natal, and needed a musician. The Brothers knew Ena well from her appearances at their Regal at Kennington and immediately asked her to go to Natal. With a big send-off, Ena sailed on the 'Athlone Castle', following a farewell broadcast on the BBC (Möller) Theatre Organ from the Jubilee Chapel, when the Announcer paid a special tribute to her. The Madingley Residential and Yacht Club at East Twickenham, of which she was a member, gave Ena a farewell party also. What with the trauma of the break-up of her marriage and all the sad good-byes, Ena was exhausted and in a highly nervous state by the time she boarded the 'Athlone Castle'. The doctor ordered her to go to bed and stay there!

Resilient Ena was soon up and about, and she and a retired dentist friend went to a fancy-dress part as 'Mustava Kummel' and Bride 'Turkish Delight'. Ena will never forget her first sight of the Table Mountain, partly obscured by a little cloud, as they approached Cape Town. The ship proceeded around the Cape, making stops at Port Elizabeth and East London, then up the coast to Durban. On arrival, she was whisked off to Durban Country Club by the O'Connor Brothers and then taken to the Palm Beach Hotel at Margate, where she was given a lovely room overlooking the sea. Ena even had a native boy to look after her. With the beautiful sunshine, Ena said it was heaven!

On March 8th, the Natal Daily News had published a photo of Ena (taken at the Odeon Blackpool), with a headline 'British organist for South Africa'. They announced that she was coming to the Union of South Africa under contract to the O'Connor Organisation for the opening of a new £100,000 Casino Theatre at Margate, and would be one of the stars of the Hibiscus Festival. A large advert welcomed all to the new Palm Beach Hotel, right on Margate Beach, grouped together with the Margate Hotel, where Ena also played, the Palm Grove and the shortly to be opened Casino. 'From London – ENA BAGA, Radio's Leading Lady Organist. Music from the Stars'.

After a couple of days, Albert O'Connor told Ena that he wanted her to meet the Mayor of Margate, and that when they met she must greet him in the customary fashion with a few words in Afrikaans. Ena had noted that the native servant always greeted her with 'Sakabourna', and when introduced to the Mayor, said 'Sakabourna'. This was apparently the worst thing she could have said! Her first faux-pas was laughed off, however. At a cocktail party at the Eden Rock Hotel she saw Jack Dowle with other guests, but he did not present himself. In the early thirties Jack Dowle played theatre organ in Maidstone, first for Granada and then for Union Cinemas at the Ritz. For Union, he visited Tunbridge Wells, Penzance, Bexleyheath, Huddersfield, St. Leonards, the Ritz Oxford and the Regal Beckenham, remaining at Beckenham with ABC into 1938. He then went to the

Regal Kingston, and, after the war, to the Gaumont Palace Wood Green, before emigrating to South Africa in 1947. His signature tune was 'Spread a Little Happiness', and we've no doubt that he did.

The Palm Beach Hotel was formerly the Belmar, and to mark its new ownership and change of name a cocktail party was held towards the end of March, 1957. The 'boss' of the family, 'Ma' O'Connor, was presented, and it was she apparently who, holidaying in Margate in 1948, took a great liking to the place and signalled the family to join her. Their aim was to acquire a string of good hotels along the coast of the state of Natal. The party was held in the Blue Room at the hotel, and 'highlight of an excellent programme of entertainment was the introduction, for the first time on the South Coast, of the celebrated London organist, Ena Baga . . . Her prowess on the Hammond organ is quite exhilerating in its *elan* and technical mastery. Appropriately, her first number was 'Blue Room' . . .

Within three months, Ena's nightly sessions at the Hammond, piano and accordion at the Palm Beach Hotel had become something of a cult for both visitors and residents, young and old. A special attraction in their Pabros Theatre at lunch-time was a free Hammond Organ recital by Ena. In July, the South Coast's 'Magnet Mag', which chronicled local events and fixtures, devoted a whole page to Ena. In poetic mood, it quoted Robert Browning 'Who hears music, feels his solitude Peopled at once', and, anonymously, 'She ran her fingers o'er the ivory keys. And shook a prelude from them as a bird shakes from its throat a song'. Praise and adulation all the way.

But, as a famous lady of the world of the cinema, Ena did not have it all her way, for, in September, Joan Crawford and her 'soft-drink king' husband, Alfred Steele, toured South Africa promoting her latest film 'The Story of Esther Costello', and opening bottling plants. At what was described as an 'Arabian-Nights-magic-carpet Press Conference', the 'Crawfords' were reunited with Ena's bosses, Albert and Sidney O'Connor. Albert took the opportunity to remind Joan Crawford that they had first met on the set of one of her earlier pictures, 'Dancing Daughters'. Her retort was 'I didn't believe there could be anyone living who'd remember that film!'

On 26th October came the opening of the O'Connors' new luxury theatre, the CASINO, and the formal opening was performed by The Mayor of Margate. The style of presentation emulated that of the famous Nat Carson shows at New York's Radio City and the Empire Leicester Square. The show began with South Africa's largest stage band, THE SKYMASTERS, followed by three variety acts, ENA BAGA 'Queen of the Organ', a presentation of Norman Hartnell's Model Gowns with South Africa's leading mannequins, and 'on the giant screen' the film 'Picnic', starring William Holden, Kim Novak and Rosalind Russell.

'All in all', said the South Coast Herald, 'the Casino's first night was a brilliant one as befitted the occasion, and was rich in promise for the future of South Coast entertainment . . . The stupendous possibilities of the giant screen were revealed in this fine first night film, the sound reproduction of which was virtually perfect . . . and greatest of all, in our opinion, the one and only Ena Baga on the Hammond organ'. The O'Connor Brothers had certainly learnt the art of entertainment in a grand style, beginning from their first major cinema project, the Regal at Kennington. A telegram received from Granada, to whom the O'Connors had sold

Royal Premiere for King and Empire! King George VI, Queen Elizabeth, and the Princesses Elizabeth and Margaret Rose attend a Royal Première at the Empire Leicester Square in the early fifties (possibly 'The Mudlark'). Florence is in the first row behind the royal party, just above the King.

the Regal, read 'We, your first born, are twenty-one this year. We welcome to the family the new addition. The Casino.' The Regal Kennington actually opened in 1937 so they were a year out. But it was a very nice thought!.

Films were not the only entertainment at the Casino. In December the choreographer Joy Shearer and her company presented 'An Evening of Spanish Ballet and Music', with the Durban Theatre Orchestra (augmented by Ena!) for the opening of the Margate Festive Season. The third item in the programme was an 'Entracte' by 'Miss Baga – Hammond Organist'.

At the end of 1957, Florence came out to join Ena for a six-months tour of the Union, and was pictured in the local press arriving at Durban and being met by Ena and Mrs. Albert O'Connor. On December 22nd, at the Casino, they joined Ann Ziegler and Webster Booth, with whom Ena had appeared at the Tower Blackpool at her first Sunday concert in 1941, for a Sunday Night entertainment. It was reported that they took the audience by storm with 'their female Rawicz and Landauer act on two pianos'.

After just over a year in Margate, Ena decided to see something of Southern Africa, and so she and Florence embarked on a tour of Rhodesia and the Union. In April, 1958, 'with a flurry of suitcases and packing cases' they left Durban for Salisbury, Rhodesia, with perhaps one of the largest and heaviest crates the railway porters had ever had to handle, labelled 'The BAGA sisters and their HAMMOND ORGAN – QUEENS OF THE KEYBOARD'. As you may imagine, the press at both Durban and Salisbury made much of that!

Their first engagement was at the Embassy Restaurant at Salisbury, 'The Rendezvous for the Discriminating' and where a Dinner Dance cost 25/-a head. The Rhodesia Herald described Ena as 'The woman with the phenomenal musical memory', which is certainly true. One evening she played the Toccata & Fugue in D Minor (Bach), Jesu, Joy of Man's Desiring, Entry of the Queen of Sheba and Handel's Water Music, followed by an Elvis Presley number. 'I didn't expect that in a pub', she said.

While at the Embassy, Ena was invited to appear in a Command Performance at the Palace Theatre Salisbury, in the presence of the Governor General, the Earl of Dalhousie and the Countess of Dalhousie, and the Federal Prime Minister, Sir Roy Welensky. It was said that the performance would imitate exactly the routine of the Royal Command Performance in London, but from the press report in the Rhodesia 'Sunday Mail' it fell rather short of this. 'Continuity was appalling', said the reporter. 'There was always a dreadful gap between the acts which would have made Val Parnell hit the ceiling if it had happened at the Palladium – which it couldn't have, of course.' Summing up, he said that the Federation's first Command Performance had 'All the appeal of a cold rice pudding'. He liked Ena Baga.

About 90 miles south-east of Salisbury is Marandellas, where old friends of Ena, Dr. and Mrs. Kay (a former nurse) ran a farm employing some 150 workers. A cable arrived from the Kays, saying 'Please come and entertain us', and so Ena and Hammond set forth for Marandellas and she spent a few extremely pleasant days on the farm. On her return to Salisbury, at a reception at the multi-racial Jameson Hotel, Ena met a Rajah and Rance. She was also introduced to the Italian Directors of the companies building the Kariba Dam, and they asked her if she would go and entertain their work force at the Dam. A lorry was dispatched for the organ and a car for Ena, and together they travelled the 200 or so miles to Lake Kariba, on the border of Northern Rhodesia. Ena described the dam as being like an enormous ant-hill. The Hammond organ was installed on the stage of the Sports Room, but the heat was absolutely terrific, the Italians making a contribution with the great fires they lit with which to cook their spaghetti! Ena always describes this chapter of her life as a 'cement and spaghetti safari'.

Down at the old Pig and Whistle! Ena entertains in the Pig & Whistle Bar of the Palm Beach Hotel, Margate, Natal, South Africa, in 1957.

All went well for the concert, except that a faulty switch silenced the organ for Ena's last item. Sabotage was not suspected. On the following night, she played in an open-air cinema, which was much cooler! Ena describes the opening of the first sluice-gate as being just like a scene from Dante's 'Inferno', which she must have accompanied many times. Equally memorable, but tragic, was a mass funeral for several of the workers who had fallen into the wet concrete.

Near the Kafue River, a tributary of the Zambezi, the Land-Rover taking her on a tour from Salisbury broke-down and Ena and her driver were stranded for a while. Through the Lufa trees Ena could see an apparent 'wall of gold'. She asked the driver what it was. 'Lions', he replied.

The man largely responsible for the development of Rhodesia was of course Cecil John Rhodes, the English imperialist who died in 1902. While staying in what was then Southern Rhodesia, Ena was taken to see Rhodes' grave and the ancient city of Zimbabwe after which the country is now named, nearly 200 miles south of Salisbury, just below Fort Victoria. She spent her weekends at the farm at Marandelas with Rex and 'Swanny' Kay. One Saturday evening just as dinner was being served, tom-toms started which was the signal that the natives were brewing beer. Ena says she was glad to see the dawn!

Having been to the borders of Northern Rhodesia at Lake Kariba, Ena was pleased to receive an invitation from the owner of the Ridgeway Hotel, Lusaka, and so she travelled to the capital of Northern Rhodesia at the beginning of August, 1958. The hotel was a beautiful place, close to the parliament building, and

Meeting the Mayor of Margate, Natal. Ena's jewellery seems to compliment the Mayor's chain of office!

Ena began her engagement there with an appearance at the Hammond at the Show Ball on August 2nd. She was kept quite busy, as she appeared daily, apart from Sunday, in the Lounge at lunchtime, at the piano and Clavioline (the electronic keyboard that imitated musical instruments and which she had first introduced at The Jolly Blacksmith a few years earlier) and at cocktail time, and on the Hammond in the Ballroom for dinner dancing from 8.30. Every Wednesday she was joined in the Ballroom by a couple of 'Joe's', Gould and Harper, for the dinner dancing; once a month she recorded programmes for the Salisbury-based Federal Broadcasting Corporation, and on several Wednesdays she introduced a popular singing guitarist, Alick Nkhata, whom she also accompanied on a recording.

The Ridgeway Hotel was popular with airforce pilots, and Ena recalls that one of them brought a pet crocodile with him which ate all the frogs in the hotel pool.

The Federal Prime Minister, Sir Roy Welensky, gave regular receptions at the Ridgeway Hotel, and Ena was invited to play for these. A musical man with a wonderful collection of records, Sir Roy's favourite piece was Toselli's 'Serenata', and Ena was always pleased to play it for him. In the 1980s, their friendship was renewed when, with friends Pat and Mary Whittet of Parkstone, she visited Sir Roy and Lady Welensksy at their home in Blandford, Dorset.

Eric Hall, who owned the Ridgeway Hotel, also directed the Jameson Hotel in Salisbury. At the end of October, 1958, Ena gave her farewell appearance at the Ridgeway and returned to Salisbury to the Jameson where, with the Hammond, piano and Clavioline, she played requests at cocktail time and during dinner. This

The Kariba Dam during construction, as visited by both Ena and Florence.

was on six days a week, Sunday being her rest day. In a series, 'Mainly for Women', the Salisbury 'Evening Standard' devoted half a page to Ena on her return and included a very nice photograph at the Hammond.

At Christmas, Ena returned to Lusaka and the Ridgeway Hotel, taking part in all the principal functions, including a Christmas Eve Gala Dance and Dinner; the Mayoress's Charity Ball; New Year's Eva Gala Supper and Ball; and the United Federal Party Ball. She also did some broad-casting over this period and a series of recitals of classical music, for which a SPECIAL Table d'hote Dinner was served for 15/-! Imagine relaxing in a comfortable hotel to a three or four course dinner, with a background of Chopin, Grieg, Debussy, Liszt, Tchaikowsky, Mendelssohn or Beethoven played by an expert pianist, all for fifteen bob! Or, today's equivalent – 75 pence!

In January, Florence again came out to South Africa, to fulfil a three-months contract at Margate, playing both piano and organ. At the beginning of March she joined Ena in Salisbury, and one of their first and most enjoyable evenings was at the Kay's tobacco farm at Marandellas, when they played accordions and 150 wildly-enthusiastic Africans responded with singing and tribal dancing.

A highlight on March 7th, 1959, was a visit by both Ena and Florence to the Kariba Dam to entertain the work-force, although for Ena this was of course a return trip. The Hammond was transported in one large packing-case, with the speaker, stool and pedalboard in the other. Precise instructions had to be given to the Kariba Transport – 'Please keep cases upright during moving – MOST

Looking particularly glamorous for the opening night of the Casino Theatre, Margate, Natal, Ena topped the bill with Anne Ziegler and Webster Booth.

Ena modelling the Persian Lamb coat, designed and made for her by Greenacres of Durban on her return to the UK from South Africa. This photo appeared in the press.

IMPORTANT'. The local press reported 'And Miss Baga is one person who cannot travel light . . . Where she goes, her Hammond Organ – a mere 1,063lb. – goes too'.

The three-day visit to Kariba, where so much mammoth construction was being carried out, had to be covered by a form signed by both sisters indemnifying the Federal Power Board against any claim arising out of death, injury or damage to property while in the vicinity of the Site of Works of the Kariba Hydro-Electric Scheme. How would one value the loss of the virtually irreplaceable Hammond, I wonder? At the end of March, Florence returned to London, and the sisters again said good-bye.

In mid-April Ena returned to South Africa and to Durban, where she opened as 'London's leading organist in her own show' at the Cumberland Hotel, playing twice nightly for dancing. 'I need the quiet of your city', she was reporting as saying, 'and specially, drought or no drought, the sight of water again. Bringing music to the bundu is one thing, but the experience of travelling through the bush where snakes and lions and myriads of creepy-crawly things are real, is quite another.' She entertained the crew of the 'Albion' when it came into port (presumably with music!), and appeared at Greenacres' Tea Lounge, daily from 17th to 29th August, playing a Lowrey electronic. Greenacres was a huge drapery store in Durban.

Having been in Southern Africa for about two-and-a-half years, Ena was beginning to feel homesick and wanting to see Mama Baga, Celeste and Beatrice. It was with much regret that she decided to come back to England. On November 14th the Natal Daily News announced 'Your last change to hear ENA BAGA, Britain's Leading Lady Organist', and the Natal Mercury head-lined 'Popular Durban Artist to Return to London'. And so, on December 1st, Ena set sail on the 'Durban Castle' for the six-weeks voyage around the East Coast of Africa, through the Red Sea, the Suez Canal, Mediterranean and home! On the day she left, the Natal Daily News carried a large, full-length photograph of Ena modelling a Persian Lamb coat for Harvey Greenacres. 'As illustrated' the advertisement read, 'Ena Baga, the famous organist, says cheerio to South Africa in a full length Persian Lamb coat in beige, trimmed detachable ranch mink'. The fur was actually designed for her by Greenacres.

The Captain of the 'Durban Castle' was named Logger Lloyd, and Ena says that he was so particular he used to test all the ship's hand-rails for dirt – daily! The first stop was at Lourenco Marques (now in Mozambique), where Ena said good-bye to the Head of Radio, David Davies, thanking him for the many broadcasts. The next port of call was Beira, and then past the mouth of the Zambezi river to the Tanganyikan Coast, calling at Dar-es-Salaam, where she was welcomed by the smell of cloves from the island of Zanzibar, and the little streets had buildings 'so close that their balconies almost touched'. Then to Kenya and Mombasa, where they stopped for a bathe at the well-known Whitesands. The ship then left the Indian Ocean for the Gulf of Aden and up through the Red Sea to the Suez Canal. On reaching Suez, the passengers were all called at 6 a.m. and told that they would be taken across the desert to Cairo in a Mercedes coach, but they didn't actually leave the ship until 9 o'clock! The Cairo hotel was in the main street, and Ena says the noise was deafening!

One of the passengers on the 'Durban Castle' was a nylon industrialist and he took Ena to the Minna House Hotel, next to the Pyramids. Seeing an advertisement for belly-dancing, Ena was keen to see this, but first she was pressed into performing on a grand piano in the Cocktail bar. As soon as she struck up, people flooded into the bar, with the result that the Manager and the local Chief of Police told her that, if she ever came to Cairo again, they would not let her go. Unavoidably (she says), Ena had too much to drink, had to retire early and missed the belly-dancing!

The next morning she embarked on her first camel-ride, but was told that it was paid for and that she should not part with any money for the experience. The Drago-man gave the camel one hell of a whack, saying 'you give me buck-shees?'. Ena meekly replied in the affirmative! That evening they dined in a restaurant opposite where the famous 'Shepheard Hotel' had been. The passengers re-embarked at Port Said, where Ena bought a radio that never worked.

The ship proceeded through the Mediterranean, along the coast of North Africa. In the Strait of Messina, opposite Sicily, a cannister of cigarettes was floated from the ship and picked up by men in small boats, who promised to send postcards home for the passengers. The ship sailed up the Italian coast, calling at Genoa , and then on to Marseille, where Ena was served with what she called 'an odd assortment of sea-foods'. After Gibraltar came the notorious Bay of Biscay, and then the first glimpse of England, Portland Bill and Durlston Head at the end of the Purbeck Hills, and Ena had tears in her eyes. A pilot came out to meet the ship, with messages from Ena's friends welcoming her home.

CHAPTER TEN

At the end of January 'Melody Maker' welcomed her home, and by the beginning of March she was back on the air at the BBC Theatre Organ. Not the ill-fated BBC Compton, opened in 1936 and destroyed the night after Ena's broadcast in 1940, but a 'giant' 27-rank theatre organ built by the American firm of Möller for Reginald Foort in 1938, with which he intended to tour the UK music halls in four custom-built vans and one smaller one. At the outbreak of the Second World War, two of the special large vans were commandeered by the RAF, but touring resumed by train with about two-thirds of the organ. This, too, became difficult, and when Foort heard that the BBC Compton had been blitzed he offered them the Möller for the duration. At first it was installed out of harm's way at the Grand Theatre Llandudno, but when hostilities ceased and it was obvious that Music Hall was in decline, the BBC bought the organ and installed it in the disused Jubilee Chapel at Hoxton, in East London. And so Ena continued broadcasting from 'The Chapel', as it became affectionately known in the theatre organ fraternity.

Ena was invited by the Cinema Organ Society to play at the Gaumont Palace Lewisham, and London area members turned up in force at the end of March to welcome her home. She began her programme at the Lewisham Compton with Clive Richardson's 'London Fantasia', which she had found to be very popular with audiences in South Africa.

For a while, Ena joined Boosey & Hawkes' in Regent Street, taking over from Frederic Curzon, one of our finest composers of light music. Born in 1899, he was musical director at a London cinema by the age of twenty and organist at the Grand Edgware Road from 1926 to 1928. He then went to the Pavilion Shepherd's Bush, where he made some 78rpm recordings, remaining for seven years and then joining Gaumont-British in London, based at the New Victoria Theatre. In 1938 he decided to concentrate on composition and arrangement of light music, and the list of titles is impressive, including the suites 'Robin Hood' and 'In Malaga'; 'Valse Joyeuse', 'Norina', 'Serenade to a Clown', 'Cantilene', 'Pantaloon', 'Overture Bouffe', and perhaps the best-known – 'The Boulevardier' and the wonderful 'Dance of an Ostracised Imp'. He died in 1973. Rarely do we hear his marvellous music today.

Boosey & Hawkes were the UK agents for the Hammond Organ Company, and when demonstrating the new Hammond 'Extravoice' organ, which had only one keyboard, Ena was heard by Max Jaffa. Max liked what he heard, and booked Ena for his next summer season at The Spa, Scarborough. Before taking off for Scarborough, where the season was due to start at the beginning of June, Ena visited not only Florence, who was in London still directing the Ritz Stockwell and the Classic Chelsea, but also Celeste and Beatrice. Celeste had been resident organist at Garon's Cinema in the Baga home town of Southend in the late forties and early fifties but, in 1960, was variety organist at the Kingsway Cinema Hadleigh, playing a six-rank Compton later presented by the cinema owners to nearby Rochford Hospital.

Back home, the 1960 summer season was spent at the Spa Scarborough with Max Jaffa. Ena is at the Hammond 'Extravoice', extreme right.

As Reginald Dixon was to the Tower Ballroom Blackpool, so Max Jaffa became synonymous with The Spa at Scarborough. Although he only appeared personally with the Spa Orchestra each evening, there were also 'Light Orchestral Concerts' at 11 each morning in the Sun Court Enclosure. For the 1960 season, the publicity included 'ENA BAGA on the Hammond Extravoice Organ'. Owing to TV commitments, the Spa Orchestra did not appear on Saturday or Sunday mornings, but Ena entertained at the Hammond and piano, with, on Sundays, Max Jaffa's wife, contralto Jean Grayston. The orchestra, with Ena, gave several live broadcasts during the season and made four appearances on television. Ena enjoyed her summer with Max Jaffa, and the sessions were not without humourous moments. One evening, Ena struck up a resounding note at the organ, lmost coinciding with 'Moaning Minnie', Scarborough's loud foghorn, the combination producing a roar of laughter from the audience. When delegates arrived at the Spa Grand Hall for the conference of Public Health Inspectors on refuse disposal, Ena included 'My Old Man's a Dustman' in her selection.

The leader of Max Jaffa's Spa Orchestra was Steven Denison, who, with brother Peter, now directs Sandford Park, a prestigious holiday centre in between Bournemouth and Swanage in Dorset. Sandford Park has a superb ballroom, designed by Peter Denison and containing not only electronic organs but a Christie theatre pipe organ that graced the nearby Regent Poole from 1927 to 1968. Installed at Sandford Park in 1977, it was enlarged and much improved, and regularly featured by resident organists Brian Sharp and Paul Roberts. In 1985 the special guest organist was Ena Baga, and you can imagine her surprise when Steven Denison greeted her with 'Remember Scarborough?' Ena has been guest organist several times since and a pleasant Sunday evening ritual has been established with the 23rd Psalm played by a trio consisting of Ena at the Christie, Brian Sharp at a Technics electronic and Steven Denison playing his violin. The console of the Christie makes a slightly unusual appearance, as a trap in the stage hinges upward to reveal the white and gold console rising on a lift.

After the summer season with Max Jaffa, Ena flew to Libya to take up her contract at Wheelus American Base, two fellow passengers being Mr and Mrs John Wayne. A slightly aggressive customs officer seemed to regard her music with some suspicion, but her explanation 'English lady come to entertain' seemed to satisfy him! She spent one night in a transit camp, billeted with a number of school teachers. Wheelus was an enormous camp, with two golf courses, chapels, restaurants, ten-pin bowling, and where you could buy anything tax-free. In contrast, "Piccolo Capri", the English camp, had only a dart-board! Gin and Whiskey in the American camp was about $2.50 a bottle, but President Kennedy wisely introduced rationing of liquor there! One need hardly wonder why the King and Queen of Tripolitania asked the Americans to build a connection from the camp to their palace!

Ena was contracted to play both in the Officers' and the NCO Clubs. Two of the first people she met were Betty Humphreys from Liverpool, employed by the U.S. Air Force and who became a life-long friend, and a ginger-headed padre with a large cigar who invited her to his room for a 'diabolical' cup of tea. Ena set about teaching him to make a proper cup of tea in the English way, as he didn't put enough in the pot and the water did not boil. (I'll bet he didn't warm the pot either!)

On January 15th, 1961, Ena celebrated her 55th birthday, and a party was arranged in the Sergeants' meeting room. Word got around the Base that a party was going on, and when someone turned up at the door with umpteen crates of booze, as Ena put it, she took flight! 'A fine hostess you are', they said next day, 'you disappeared!'. Apparently things got a bit out of hand, as the 'Snowdrops', as the white-caps were known, had to break up the party.

Wheelus was the biggest American Air Base outside the USA. On St. Patrick's Day, March 17th, when tucking in to corned-beef and cabbage at one of the restaurants, Ena noticed that the potatoes had been tinted green, in company with all the traffic lines!

After six months at Wheelus, Ena returned home to England, to find a letter from the Cumberland Hotel, Durban, asking her to go back. Five months previously, at the beginning of 1961, Florence had made her annual pilgrimage to the State of Natal, playing Hammond for dancing at the Cumberland and demonstrating the new Wurlitzer 'Side Man', a cabinet with speaker that automatically played any rhythm in strict tempo, including the Waltz, cha-cha-cha-, foxtrot, samba, tango, rumba, etc. Florence was unable to stay long because of her business commitments, so the Cumberland management begged Ena to go back. Apart from summer seasons, there was little work in the UK at the time, so Ena decided to make her home in South Africa and went back to Durban on a small, friendly ship, the 'City of Exeter'. The ship ran into a tornado off the South

Florence at the Cumberland Hotel, Durban, playing Hammond with 'Sideman' percussive unit.

What shall we do with the drunken sailor? Yvonne Mehro and Florence entertaining at the Broadstairs Bandstand.

West African coast and, although Ena's bunk was fitted with 'fiddles' (wooden racks) to prevent her from falling out, she eventually did so just as the ship hit the pier at Cape Town!

At a fancy-dress ball on board, Ena admits to having had a drink or two, appearing as a wandering minstrel with accordion. The next morning, she had to play for the church service and moved the piano so that she could see the 'ladies'.

The next ports of call after Cape Town were Port Elizabeth and East London, and Ena will always remember the latter. An importer of leather goods invited all 40 passengers to lunch at his home. After lunch, they were all taken in cars to a large field with trenches full of fruit and two large barriers, behind which was the sea, as calm as a mill-pond. She also encountered there a King Elephant, the largest she had ever seen, and his tribe. After East London came Durban, where she was met by the O'Connors and taken to the Cumberland Hotel, where she opened with 'London Fantasia', with the help of flashing lights from the manager and bomb noises from Ena. With memories of the blitz, her 'London Fantasia' had even men crying, so she had to repeat this every night.

At the beginning of 1962, while Ena was still in Durban, 'Able-Seaman' Florence de Jong joined the company of R.M.S. Queen Mary, the first woman musician to do so. After a few crossings back and forth, she felt rather exhausted and telephoned Ena in South Africa. 'How would you like to see New York?', she said. Florence had informed Bandleader Geraldo, who held the musical agency for the

Hooked-on classics? Ena looking happy aboard the Hammond on RMS 'Queen Mary' in 1962. Note 'Side-man' percussive unit in foreground and the seat hooked to the wall for rough weather.

Cunard ships that Ena was more than capable of doing the job, and so it was agreed that Ena should take over in March, 1962. Following a physical examination at Cable Street, E1, she became a registered seaman, and she completed six trips on the Queen Mary. In early spring the weather in the mid-Atlantic was rough, with the waves reaching the windows of the Main Lounge under the bridge. The Queen Mary was notorious for its rolling motion in heavy seas, even with stabilisers. Entertainment and facilities on the ship were fantastic, including Swimming Pool and Keep-fit classes, record concerts of classical music, newsbroadcasts, dinner music from the 'Queen Mary String Orchestra' and dancing from 10 to midnight with the Dance Orchestra. There was also a daily movie in the afternoon and evening.

Ena's first playing session was at cocktail time in the Main Lounge, and as it was very rough the Hammond was clamped to the floor. In the middle of her performance and with the lounge full of passengers nausea began to overtake her and she realised she was about to be sick. In the nick of time, the orchestra appeared, and she made a wild dash to the back of the stage and an empty champagne bucket. After that terrible experience, Ena was given an injection that took away all feeling of sea-sickness, but the stewards always put out a champagne bucket just the same!

After the cocktail hour, Ena played for a Bingo session each evening and she also provided the music for afternoon tea-dances. On Sunday mornings she played for

Florence meets George Thalben-Ball on board RMS Alcantra.

both Captain's and the Roman Catholic services, which made for a long day as her evening sessions did not finish before 10 pm. As she put it, she had the rest of the day to herself! Interesting passengers on the 'Q.M.' included the King of the Gold Coast and his entourage; John Mills and his family; one of the Directors of Chappells of Bond Street; and a large number of friends in the advertising world. The Chief Steward, named Pritchard, introduced Ena to a recording of the music from Richard Rodgers' musical 'No Strings', the score of which included some pretty songs, for example, the title tune and 'The Sweetest Sounds', which has long been one of Ena's favourites. She went to the dress rehearsal of the West End production, but unfortunately the show was not a success in the UK.

In June, 1962, and after six round trips, Ena decided that she had had enough – seamen's pay was not that good anyway! The following month, she was contacted by her agent asking her to go to Broadstairs to team up with Yvonne Mehro at the Bandstand, as her husband, Ted Farley, the organist in their double act, had suddenly died just after the season had commenced.

Edward Farley was a theatre organist for many years, playing for silent films at the Cinedrome Plymouth and at the Royalty Richmond, Surrey, up to 1930. He then opened the Compton theatre organs at the Richmond Kinema (now Odeon), the Gaumont Palace Lewisham and the Coliseum Harrow. From 1935 he toured Union Cinemas, but joined ABC at the Regal York in 1937. From 1939 he spent a year or two at other York cinemas as organist/manager, followed by Brixton Astoria, Leeds and Southend. In 1952 he teamed up with vocalist Yvonne Mehro, whom he later married, and together they appeared at various seaside resorts running the show at Broadstairs Bandstand from 1960 until his sudden death.

The season recommenced at the beginning of July, with Yvonne Farley as vocalist and hostess and Ena at the Compton Theatrone electronic organ, entertaining audiences in all kinds of weather. The programme varied from 'Music Light and Bright' every afternoon and on Sunday evenings; 'In Holiday Mood', described as The Happy Family Show, every evening, with talent contests, twist and talent finals night, and a Children's Night. Every Monday evening there was a 'Holiday Princess' contest for ladies; every Tuesday a 'Holiday Fashion Parade'; and every Monday afternoon a 'Children's King & Queen Contest', for which Yvonne made the dresses. The final 'King & Queen' for the 1962 season were pictured on the front page of the Broadstairs & St. Peter's Mail, hand-in-hand with Ena and Yvonne.

All that sounds like very hard work, and a little time off for recreation was needed from time to time. One Saturday afternoon Ena was taken to Pegwell Bay to see the Hovercraft terminus. When she got back, there was a message to say that her eldest sister Celeste was dead. Having acted as variety organist at the Kingsway Hadleigh in 1960, Celeste had followed Florence for the summer season at Herne Bay Bandstand, where her performances proved very popular. In fact, her services were so much appreciated that the Secretary of the Hotel, Restaurant & Guest House Association for Herne Bay presented her with a bouquet at the end of her season in September. Unfortunately this was her last engagement, as she died on August 1st, 1962, on Florence's birthday. Yvonne having lost a husband and Ena having lost a sister, there were many tears behind the scenes that summer. I regret that I did not have the chance to meet Celeste Baga. William Davies said that she had great talent.

During the winter, Ena was to be found demonstrating for Hammond (UK), touring the North of England, Channel Islands (where she has often returned), Scotland and Ireland. In Scotland, she visited fishing towns on the Grampian coast. At Buckie, where she saw girls gutting the herrings, the audience wanted hymns. 'With or without tremulant?' Ena asked, but they did not mind, so she played hymns with trems on. The 'Granite City' of Aberdeen had icy pavements, and at the smoking sheds Ena saw the trawlers being filled with ice. In Glasgow she was taken to see Loch Lomond and Ben Lomond. In Ireland, she went to see the famous Mountains of Mourne, and to meet Louise Macdonald at Hollywood, near Belfast, where Louise was teaching the piano and where she and her husband ran an antique shop.

Louise Macdonald was yet another lady theatre organist. She trained at the Royal Manchester College of Music, and her first organ post was at the Tonic Cinema, Bangor, Northern Ireland. After 4 years there, she was appointed to the Gaumont Palace Plymouth, in 1945. Two years later she returned to Northern Ireland, to the Classic Belfast, going back to the Tonic in 1952. She gave some fine broadcasts from the Tonic, making effective use of the Melotone (electronic) unit. Her broadcasts were usually for the BBC Regional Home Service in Northern Ireland, but if the wind was in the right direction 'every little breeze . . . whispered Louise' in the South, if a little faintly!

For the summer of 1963, Ena went 'home' to Southend-on-Sea. 'The Stage &

Television Today' reported: 'The old "wedding-cake" bandstand on the Cliffs at Southend housed all the famous military bands. When it was replaced by the Bandstage, it became the home of orchestras . . . This year, for the first time, there is Melody Mixture, which brings back memories of variety bills . . . Ena Baga, of the well-known family of musicians in Southend, proves just how wide and rich the range of a Hammond organ can be, and backs the other acts . . .' Ena stayed with her school-friend of some 45 years standing, Nora Mingay. Meanwhile, Florence was demonstrating for the John Compton company and spent the summer on the Sun Terrace at the Lido Margate, where Ena had spent the end of the previous season!

For 1964, the venue was Paignton, South Devon, which then still had a theatre and two cinemas. The cinemas were showing Bugs Bunny and Teenage Franken-stein, but if you wanted family entertainment your rendezvous was the Summer Pavilion, where Ena provided 'Morning Music', 'Quiz Bingo', 'Paignton Holiday Girl' talent competitions and "Sunday Serenade'. It's not clear if she took part in the 'Wrestling' on Monday evenings! While at Paignton, she took tea with Terence Dene, who was living in a nearby hotel. Terence, a friend from Gaumont British days, began his career in the West End of London, at the Pavilion Shaftesbury Avenue and Madame Tussad's Cinema, Marylebone. In 1933 he went to the Carlton Upton Park, an unusual cinema cleverly constructed within the quadrangle of an institutional school, using the existing buildings for side and rear walls and stage. In 1934, Dene opened a Compton at the Gaumont Palace Chadwell Heath, which had not only an illuminated console but a spectacular fan that opened behind the console as it arose from the orchestra pit. In 1948, he followed the well-known Al Bollington at the Paramount/Odeon Tottenham Court Road, transferring to management for Odeon at Croydon, Putney and Leicester Square, where he often 'took tea' with organist Gerald Shaw.

In 1965, Ena enjoyed a summer season at what must have been one of the windiest theatres in the UK, the Knightstone at Weston-Super-Mare, built on a short promenade between two stretches of water. She shared the bill with pianist Mrs. Mills and comedian Ted Rogers, who thought he would like to play a round of golf with Ena. Significantly, perhaps, the lady captain introduced them to a couple of men for a game of bridge instead! While at Weston, Ena took tea with BBC singer Margery Avis and met up with Bryan Rodwell, who was with the Vernon Adcock Show at the Rozel. Bryan is a brilliant musician with an amazing keyboard technique. He began his career at the age of 16 at the Forum Southampton for ABC, followed by the Central Kidderminster, when there was an interruption for his national service. He returned to ABC at the Ritz Hereford, but joined Granada as variety organist at East Ham in 1951, remaining there until 1958. He then went 'up-market' to the Theatre Royal Drury Lane, followed by Granada TV and several years with the Vernon Adcock Show until, like other organists, he became 'mine host' (at the Walnut Tree, Old Mixon, near Weston, in 1967). Since then, he has demonstrated for Hammond, both in Chicago and the UK, and for Rodgers organs. He has also toured with Edmund Hockridge, as his accompanist at the piano. Meeting him at a society concert at the Granada Harrow, he said in that mild Yorkshire accent that he never completely lost, 'Cum and see the latest addition to the family'. There, gurgling in pram in the aisle was 'the latest addition'. 'Mind you', Bryan said, 'we're not going to have any more. We found out what's causin' it.'

During 1965 Ena was also touring for Hammond (UK). Her travels took her to Palma, Majorca; Vigo, in the north-west corner of Spain and where the owner of the music shop had nine sons; Barcelona, where Ena was taken to an interesting restaurant for an Andalucian meal; Bilbao in the north-east, and to Madrid by 'plane over the mountains. The flight to Madrid was delayed and Ena took a meal at the airport restaurant, where the menu included 'Rape- American style'. She didn't try it. In Madrid the venue for the Hammond concert was a hall in the college and the organ was the latest model, the X77. Ena's Latin American medley brought the house down, and a Spanish lady said that she 'played like an angel'; Ena was presented with a silver salver to mark her visit.

The international 'Hammond Times' for December 1965 included a two-page biography and photograph of Ena under the title "My World of Music".

Able Seaman De Jong of R.M.S. 'Queen Mary'.

CHAPTER ELEVEN

One of the most interesting and prettiest places to visit is the Isle of Man, and it was there that Ena spent the summer of 1966. The Hammond was delayed by a strike of seamen but an alternative electronic instrument of sorts was found for her, which Ena says arrived in a cardboard box. The venue was Bradda Glen, near Erin, which now has the distinction of being served by the only remaining steam railway line on the Island. Ena very much enjoyed her stay on the Isle of Man, which we both think is beautiful.

One evening, the door of the hall burst open and a huge man with a dog and a vast bunch of flowers, which he later presented to Ena, settled himself into the front row. At the end of the concert, he asked Ena to take a drink with him at her hotel, and word sped around the Island that she was being wooed by the local farmer!

At one time the Isle of Man did actually house a couple of theatre organs; one was at the Picture House, Douglas, and was a Compton that replaced a Jardine 'straight' organ opened by the great Quentin Maclean; the other, also a Compton, was at the Regal and opened by the well-known George Tootell. Both were removed in 1963/4 not long before Ena visited the Island, but the Isle of Man now has its first Wurlitzer, installed at the Summerland complex.

At the end of the season, Ena returned to London and her flat at Hammersmith. She was immediately asked to join the staff of a new organ and piano venture, The Sound of Music, at Chiswick, teaching and demonstrating, and where she spent six happy years.

And what had Florence been doing since 'basking' (and that's likely to be the wrong word) on Margate's Lido Sun Terrace in 1963? Well, Broadstairs Bandstand couldn't do without a Baga for more than one season, and, Ena having stepped in for Ted Farley in 1962, Florence joined Yvonne Farley for the seasons from 1964 to 1966. Every weekday evening, Yvonne and Florence, 'Two in Harmony', presented a show with a different emphasis, and every afternoon and Sunday evening, a show of both music and song, 'Musical Rendezvous'. The repertoire was wide, including everything from Tchaikowsky's No. 1 Piano concerto and Schubert's Serenade through opera, musical comedy and waltzes to popular songs on the current hit list. And the audiences were still singing 'Hullo Broadstairs', by the late Ted Farley.

After her third summer season with Yvonne Farley, Florence was offered a similar post to Ena, at the newly-opened 'Sound of Music' at Maidenhead, Berkshire, but returned to Broadstairs for the summer of 1967. In that year, she made her first LP Album, back at the New Gallery Regent Street, where she was resident for 13 years from 1925 and where she had often recorded at 78rpm. Volume 4 in a series 'Unit Organ Parade', it had the title "Memories" and included Drigo's 'Serenade', a Polonais by Chopin, Debussy's 'Clair de Lune', 'The Swan' (Saint-Saens), the Handel Largo and Sibelius' 'Finlandia'. 'The Swan', from 'The Carnival of the Animals', had previously been recorded on film by Florence at the Regal Walton-on-Thames for Pathé Pictorial.

In 1961 the 10 rank Wurlitzer had been removed from the Metropole Victoria and placed in store, as a result of the installation of a Todd-AO screen, a new orchestra pit and the removal of 500 seats from the front stalls. This organ had a connection with a lady, but not an organist – a well-known actress. In 1944, Noel Coward had adapted one of his one-act playlets from 'Tonight at 8.30' ('Still Life') for a film, 'Brief Encounter', which he persuaded David Lean to produce. It turned out to be an excellent film, starring Celia Johnson and Trevor Howard strongly supported by Stanley Holloway and Joyce Carey. At one point, the heroine, Laura, and her newly-found doctor friend visit the cinema and, in the interval, up rises a Wurlitzer console with the 'cellist from the nearby café, played by Irene Handel. The scene was shot in the Metropole, with the organ music dubbed in by the resident organist at the time, James Whitebread.

While the Metropole Wurlitzer was stored, the console was destroyed by fire. When it was removed to Buckingham Town Hall, the console from a similar Wurlitzer at the Troxy Stepney removed in 1961 when that theatre became the London Opera Centre, was connected. The organ was re-opened at Buckingham in May 1963 by Robinson Cleaver, William Davies and Jackie Brown. It was later removed to Worthing Assembly Hall, where in 1991 it celebrated its tenth anniversary, but we shall come back to that. Soon after the opening at Buckingham the organ was chosen by Concert Recording of California, USA, for one side of Ena Baga's first album, the other half being recorded on a C3 Hammond installed in the Town Hall for the purpose. This first LP of Ena's was a great success, to the extent that it was reissued on the Crystal label under the title 'Champagne for Two' (sparkling music for two organs); one of the items on the record and composed by Ena herself.

Another organ removed because of wide-screen installation was that in the Gaumont Palace Birmingham, this time a 10-rank Compton, which was installed in the Abbey Hall at Abingdon, Oxfordshire, and opened there in 1966 by George Blackmore, Noel Briggs and Jackie Brown. Ena's second LP was made there for Concert Recording soon after the opening and was a selection of Christmas music under the title 'Joy To The World', including four tracks on Hammond organ. In the ten years from 1967, Ena made no less than 12 albums, mostly on various Hammond models but including two with Florence of piano themes for silent movies and one at the Odeon Leicester Square of the music of Richard Rodgers. Richard Rodgers himself wrote to Teddy Holmes, of Chappell & Co, who sponsored the record, as follows: 'The Ena Baga record arrived and I have played it. I must tell you that ever since my boyhood I have been unable to listen comfortably to organ music. This is because I used to skip school in the afternoons and go to the movies. They always were accompanied by an organ and I suppose my resistance to this instrument is a carry-over of boyhood guilt. This does not prevent my recognizing the excellence of the Baga record and I am sure, and I hope, it will be an enormous success. Thank you so much for letting me have it. Fondest regards. (signed) Dick'

In mid-1967, Florence was returning by boat from her annual visit to South Africa and was introduced to the then Rhodesian Prime Minister Ian Smith, on his way to Cape Town. He asked Florence for a dance, and, on telling her how fond he

Florence enjoying the Farewell Cruise of RMS 'Queen Mary' in 1967 – this time as a passenger!

was of organ music, Florence offered the Premier a recital. Ian Smith listened to her for two hours, and later sent her a signed photograph. While Florence was resting and recuperating from her travels, Ena had to get up at 5am to broadcast from the Gaumont State Kilburn. Programming on the 'Light' began at 6.55 am on a Sunday morning with 'Christian words and music', followed at 7 by the weather report and the news, after which came Ena at the organ.

Later in the year, both sisters were the guests of honour, together with Mr and Mrs Fredric Bayco, at the third Cinema Organ Society Annual Dinner in London.

In September, Florence was the first lady organist to play in concert at the Abbey Hall, and the 'Oxford Mail' went to town with a photograph and a potted biography. The photo was taken on board the 'Queen Mary', which the Mail mentioned was at that time making its last voyage across the Atlantic. In 1987 I saw her resting at Long Beach, California, doing duty as a hotel and tourist attraction.

From 1964 to 1967, Ena took part in "Music's Most Glorious Voice',continuous 20 minute recitals in the Hammond Organ Theatre, Empire Hall, Olympia, presented by Hammond (UK) Ltd. Three organists, Ena, Keith Beckingham an Roy Jevons, took turns to give the recitals and there were three Hammond models featured: Model M.102 (spinet); Model 2000 (Chord organ); and E.100, then one of the newest in the Hammond range and described as having a 'dramatic new theatre sound . . . that gives even the beginner the professional touch". Keith Beckingham, in his early twenties, had appeared at theatre organs since the age of fourteen, including his 'local', the Regal Beckenham. He was the star of Hammond touring shows as far afield as the Soviet Union and South Africa, and, every

What no audience? Ena demonstrates for Hammond (UK) at the Ideal Home Exhibition, 1965.

March, appeared at the Hammond Organ Theatre in the Ideal Home Exhibition with Ena. One year younger, Roy Jevons had been playing since age thirteen and, following a spell in cabaret clubs and dance halls, he joined the Hammond Company as demonstrator in 1966.

Both ladies appeared at the Buckingham Town Hall Wurlitzer in 1968, Ena in March and Florence in June. At this time, both had changed their signature tunes, Ena's being her own 'Bagatelle' and Florence appropriately adopting 'My Song Goes Round The World'. Ena's programme included Friedman's 'Slavonic Rhapsody' and Rossini's overture to 'William Tell', while Florence included the Toccata from 'Suite Gothique'' by Boellmann.

The week before Florence appeared at Buckingham, Ena was in concert at Southampton Guildhall, playing the magnificent Compton with twin consoles; one concert, one theatre. Her programme included two pieces by Albert Ketelby, the first being 'In A Monastery Garden'. Searching for the bird-whistle toe-piston with her foot, she hit the very loud klaxon by mistake! Nothing daunted, Ena found the bird-whistle, and explained to the audience that there was a noisy road outside the monastry! On a return visit, Ena's concert was to be followed in the evening by a military band. Escorted by her friend, George Muteaux, they found when they arrived home that George had mistakenly picked up the band conductor's case containing his uniform for the evening performance. Ena at once telephoned the Guildhall to apologise, but the conductor apologised to Ena for the inconvenience.

Early in 1969, the Academy Cinema in London's Oxford Street presented its first season of Buster Keaton silents. Opened in January 1913 as the 'Picture House', it became established in the thirties as an eminent art house, and, as Allen Eyles and Keith Skone say in 'London's West End Cinemas', it had 'come to be trusted by its audiences and (could) make a success of films that would have dubious prospects anywhere else." Piano accompaniment for the silent seasons was provided by 'Miss Florence de Jong, Miss Ena Baga, Mr Michael Steer and Mr Stanley Kilburn', with Florence as the M.D. A second season was arranged for Christmas, 1970, and they continued each year (also featuring Douglas Fairbanks films) until the Academy unfortunately closed in 1986.

In April 1970, the Cinema Organ Society presented a Theatre Organ Festival at the ABC Cinema (former Regal) Torquay and the Top Rank Club (former Palladium/Odeon) Paignton. Arranged by organist Don Knights and COS South-west Secretary Kenneth Butterfield, the Festival had become an annual event with three concerts and a dinner, making for a very pleasant week-end in Torbay. Together with Don Knights and Noel Briggs, Ena was the star guest. While in the south-west, Ena appeared at Dunster, near Minehead.

'Partner to Valentino' was the heading in the Women's Guardian on August 7th, above a picture of Florence at her piano and with the famous white streak very much in evidence. Jane Alexander reported that the most enthusiastic response for any of the varied events at the 'New Universities Festival' at Lancaster was reserved for silent films with piano accompaniment by Florence de Jong. The main feature was Valentino in 'Son of the Sheik' 'and Miss de Jong's piano joyously punctuated the whole thing with clever allusive tunes'. There was also Laurel and Hardy and Charlie Chaplin in the programme, all immensely enjoyed by students and older academics alike. Florence was treated like a movie queen herself, and during the final ovation the student organiser presented Florence with a bouquet 'and kissed her fervently, boyishly on the cheek. It seemed a proper salute for an endearing performance.'

In November, the London Evening Standard also took up the theme, with Fiona MacCarthy stating 'Everyone worships Florence de Jong these days. She is part of the great silent film revival . . . when she had thought that her career was long since over, Florence de Jong is more in demand than ever. She plays constantly at the National Film Theatre and on Friday (Nov. 6th) accompanies D. W. Griffith's monumental 'Birth of a Nation' at the gala performance at the Regent in Brighton.

On November 22nd both ladies appeared in concert at the Abbey Hall, Abingdon for the Mayor's Annual Charity Concert, and argued all the way as to who had been responsible for bringing Ena to the New Gallery in 1926'. Ena was still using 'Bagatelle' for a signature tune but Florence was signing on with Papa Baga's 'Passing Thoughts' again. After the interval, it was 'Two in Harmony' with Ena at the piano and Florence at the organ, ending with community singing.

A week later, Ena was with two other ladies at the Paramount/Odeon Manchester, topping the bill at the Wurlitzer with Doreen Chadwick, soprano Enid Powell and the Collyhurst Girls Choir. Doreen Chadwick had followed Ena at the Oxford Corner House in 1951, but her career began (after organ lessons at the Palladium in her home town of Pontypridd) on a Compton Theatrone electronic organ at the Rex Aberdare in 1939. In 1941 she joined Granada at Tooting, touring the circuit, until 1944 when she went to ABC and the Savoy

Leicester. From 1946 to 1949 she was at the Ritz Richmond playing its beautiful 8-rank Wurlitzer. After her short spell at Lyons' Corner House in succession to Ena, Doreen became resident at the Market Hotel Oldham, Lancs, later moving to the Magnet Hotel, which she ran with her husband, Len. Doreen returned to the theatre organ for two months in 1959 to play preludes for 'South Pacific' at the Gaumont Manchester. She is still much in demand in the 1990's as a concert artist on both pipe and electronic, and her swinging, lively style has many admirers. The Theatrone on which she made her first public appearance is now in the Isle of Wight where it will form the basis of a museum.

On 22nd December, 1970, Ena, Florence and Beatrice were all going out to dinner to celebrate Christmas, when the awful news came through that Beatrice had been found dead in her flat at Victoria. She had apparently just lit a cigarette, so her death must have been sudden and swift. Ena obviously did not feel like merry-making, but I persuaded her to come to my party on the 27th, which I hope relieved the sadness a little.

CHAPTER TWELVE

When Florence was resident at the New Gallery she occasionally visited other theatres on the Gaumont-British circuit. Shortly after the beautiful Gaumont Palace opened at Wood Green, North London, it was visited by Ena, Stanley Tudor and Florence, all making a guest appearance for one week. One evening during Florence's week the lift stuck right at the top, and Florence had to be ignominiously lifted down at the end of her interlude. The 12-rank Compton was removed from Wood Green in 1966 and re-opened at Twickenham College of Technology in March, 1969. An early visitor, in January 1971, was Ena, and I notice that she included 'In A Monastry Garden' in her programme. I hope she didn't hit the klaxon again! One of those instrumental in obtaining the organ for Twickenham was Bill Hiscock, and he and his wife Joan became good friends of Ena, always ready to help her with transport when needed. Bill must have been sorry to see the organ leave the College in the late seventies. It popped up again at the Thorngate Hall Gosport, where it was opened by John Mann in 1981 and where it sounds better than ever.

One of the longest running shows must have been 'Tuesday at the Dome', a very popular variety evening at the Dome Brighton. For a few years I lived and worked at Brighton, and the compère for the show was one 'Clifford Rawson', actually Tommy Cheetham of the Private Hire department at Southdown Motor Services. In those days, Borough Organist Douglas Reeve always filled the organ spot, also taking part in the obligatory quiz at the end of the show. I remember one night he knocked the tin of questions down the organ console, and when he dropped half-a-crown prize money on the stage, Clifford called out 'Hold onto the Money!'.

Born in Brighton, Douglas Reeve became assistant to H. Goddard at the Savoy in that town when only 14. He was discovered by Reginald Foort, when visiting the Brighton Regent, and toured County Cinemas in an Eton collar and what he describes as a 'bum-freezer jacket' as the 'Wonder Boy Organist'. From 1934 to 1938, he was based at the Regal Golders Green, doubling as variety organist at the Orpheum Temple Fortune. After a short period in the Army at Aldershot, where he married the youngest recruit to the ATS by candle-light – there was a power cut – he was appointed Borough Organist to Brighton (in 1941), a post that, at the time of writing, he still holds after 50 years.

In 1971, Douglas was also managing the Dome and producing the Tuesday night variety shows, usually with guest organists. Ena and I went down to Brighton (in all weathers) for these shows, and during 1971, she appeared as guest organist on July 6th and August 3rd. Douglas Reeve put the Dome theatre/concert organ on the air, on wax and very much on the map, and when I lived in Brighton it was almost impossible to find a spare seat at his 'Pack Up Your Troubles' organ concerts. Not for nothing has he earned the title of 'Mr. Brighton'.

On 11th August, Florence and Ena both accompanied the evening silents at the Academy, Ena creeping in and taking over from Florence at the piano without

Ena demonstrates for Chappells of Bond Street in 1972.

anyone noticing. Some of the audience were mystified, having seen Florence walk across to the piano, only to see Ena there when the lights went up!

Another Brightonian is John Mann, one of the most popular organists in the country. He joined forces with Ena at Taverham Hall, a boys' school six miles from Norwich, for a concert on October 17th. The organ at Taverham was installed in the school gymnasium (without its glass surround!) and was a 6-rank Compton with Melotone Unit from the Regal Harrogate, removed to Norwich in 1968/69. Enlarged by two ranks, it was sold in 1979 to Mr. and Mrs. Stiff at Mere Farm, Haughley, Suffolk, where it is presented in concert by Dudley Savage. Dudley loves that particular organ, as it is akin to the one at the Royal Plymouth, which he broadcast for thirty years or more. Apart from the organ, the one thing I remember about Taverham is their home-brewed beer, which they wisely did not serve in larger than half-pint glasses!

In 1971, Florence was appointed Musical Director to the National Film Theatre, where she was assisted by Ena, Stanley Kilburn and Arthur Dulay. Such a prestigious appointment at the age of 75 was a great tribute to Florence's ability!

In 1972, Ena ended her six years with 'The Sound of Music' at Chiswick and became part-time teacher and demonstrator for Chappell of Bond Street. The Duchess of Kent was a frequent visitor there and liked to talk about music. Edward Heath also put in an appearance, but with a smile and a shake of the shoulders he declined to try the latest grand piano. In March we went to the beautiful city of Bath, where the 9-rank Wurlitzer from the Regent Brighton had been installed in the Pavilion and opened the year previously by Ernest Broadbent, the last resident at the Regent. In July, Ena and Florence played for the Cinema Organ Society at the Granada Sutton. This theatre had been built by Florence's second husband, Lou Morris, in 1934, and received a 10-rank Compton with stylish illuminated console from the Prince's Theatre Shaftesbury Avenue (now the Shaftesbury), where it had been installed for a short time in 1933. Originally the Plaza, the Sutton theatre had quickly been acquired by Granada and renamed about 1945. The manager in 1972 was Mike Ramsden, one of Granada's best.

'The dust covers will be taken off the organ at the State Cinema in Grays on Sunday for a special recital by Florence de Jong – the widow of the man who built the Ritz' . . . said the Thurrock Gazette on December 8th, 1972, under a picture of Florence rehearsing at the console with manager Derek Smeedon in the background. And that's what caused the trouble! On a wet and windy Sunday, the three of us travelled to Grays and, after rehearsals, I left Ena and Florence to rest in the manager's office. I was compèring the show, and at five minutes to three went to collect Florence. She was not in the best of moods and, after my introduction from the stage, showed indignation because I had said that she was the 'assistant' to Jack Courtnay at the New Gallery, rather than the 'orchestral organist'. I was puzzled by her attitude, but when I got back to the office, Ena, defiantly smoking a cigarette with legs firmly apart, said 'we've had a bull and cow!' The 'bull and cow', or row, was about the publicity which was mainly about Florence and hardly mentioned Ena. It was thankfully smoothed over before we started the journey home.

It should be said that both ladies were made of stern stuff, and in no way did their 'bull and cow' affect their performances. Like the true professionals they were born to be, they always gave of their best in public, even when racked with arthritis as Florence once was. I had to stand behind her and rub her back all the way through rehearsal. Once in front of the audience, they forgot their differences (and sometimes aches and pains) and entertained for all their worth like the best of troupers.

I remember one other little squabble, at the New Gallery. The producer of the initial series of 'The Organist Entertains' BBC Radio 2 weekly programme was the efficient and meticulous Chris Morgan, the programme being presented by the man who inspired the series, Robin Richmond. One afternoon in the early seventies, after a good lunch in the BBC Club Salad Bar at The Langham (where Chris, Robin and I often met), we went down to the New Gallery for an afternoon's recording by Ena and Florence. They recorded about six pieces, e.g. 'Cornish Rhapsody' and 'Warsaw Concerto', both of which were included in a BBC Record, 'More Hits from The Organist Entertains', selected by Robin and produced by Chris and issued in 1971. After one 'take' that Chris felt was a little too long for the programme, Florence called up from the Wurlitzer 'Ena, you must cut some of your cadenzas'. 'I'm NOT cutting anything' came the reply from the grand piano. Professional jealousy – even from close sisters.

Later in the afternoon the sychronisation of the two artists was a little awry, causing Ena to say sharply 'You watch me – I'm the important one in this!'. Back came the reply 'I can't watch you, and the organ, and the music and my feet!'. Robin smiled and lent across to me. 'Aren't they a couple of old darlings', he said.

In 1971 Florence had paid a return visit to Guernsey, her first for many years, to play for the local Hammond Organ Society. The Guernsey Evening Press & Star

'Extravorganza 1973' at the Opera House Jersey, presented by the Channel Islands Hammond Organ Society. Florence and Ena in concert with (on the right) Stanley King and George Blackmore. The Jersey Ladies Choir also took part. (photo: Evening Post, Jersey).

had gone to town, with a large picture of Florence at a Hammond at the Royal Hotel and with mention of Florence's long and happy association with the island and happy memories of her guest appearances at the Regal Guernsey in the late 1930s.

In February 1973 it was Jersey's turn, and the Jersey Branch of the Channel Islands Hammond Organ Society staged 'EXTRAVORGANZA '73' at the Jersey Opera House, with Ena and Florence as the stars of the show, supported by Stanley King of Hammond Organs and The Jersey Ladies Choir. Florence and Ena were of course well remembered in the Channel Islands for their visits to the Guernsey Regal; and Stanley King, who was promoting showcases for Hammond Organs (UK), was well-known in Jersey from a successful season at the Forum Cinema and from his appearance in the 1970 'Extravorganza' with Robin Richmond. Stanley's style and sense of humour has won him many admirers, and of his recordings on Kimball Xanadu Organ, 'King in Concert', has been described as 'The ultimate in keyboard technology . . . making it difficult to believe that it is only one man and an organ.' He now lives and works in Canada but pays an occasional visit to our shores.

Early in 1973 The Guardian devoted half their woman's page to Florence and Ena and the art of silent film accompaniment, under the heading 'Keeping up with the Keystone Cops'. Reporter Jane Watts interviewed Florence at her Kensington Church Street flat, and Ena 'all in pink under her new mink', appeared during the

Breezy Brighton! Ena and the Author on one of their frequent visits to Brighton for a guest appearance in 'Tuesday at the Dome'.

Guardian Angels! Florence and Ena being interviewed by Janet Watts of 'The Guardian' in 1972.

chat. 'Before I could request it, the two had plonked themselves on the piano stool and launched into a vigorous rendering of Chopin's Minute Waltz, 'Tico Tico' and 'Brazil'. 'I wish I was there'' said Florence, gold earings jiggling, arms energetic through her black chiffon sleeves'. Florence admitted to having one unfulfilled wish – to get an organ into the National Film Theatre. A wish that remained unfulfilled, regrettably, although a Wurlitzer was later ear-marked for the NFT's permanent Museum of the Moving Image.

One ambition that was fulfilled was an appearance on BBC Radio's 'Desert Island Discs', as on Saturday 7th April 1973 'Florence de Jong, cinema organist and pianist, (discussed) with Roy Plomley the records she would take to a Desert Island'. The Radio Times carried a photo of Florence at the piano, superimposed on a sketch of a deserted island complete with wind-up gramophone, entitled 'Able Seaman de Jong', a hark-back to her days on the Queen Mary. 'I've been on too many ships in rough seas to try escaping on a raft', she said.

From the end of June until mid-July, the Hillingdon Theatre Arts Club staged a Summer Arts Festival at Ickenham, one of the events of which was an evening with Florence and Ena, talking about their careers as cinema musicians. The ladies were very highly regarded at the Hillingdon Theatre Arts Club, later Compass Theatre, and had a long and happy association with the club and in particular with the producer (and Jack of all trades), John Sherrat.

1973 was the year in which, under the auspices of the Kodak Award Scheme, a young man named David Furnham made an interesting film tracing the development of cinemas and cinema-going from the fairground bioscope, village hall and seaside pier to the super picture palaces of the late 20s and 1930s. The film, 'An Acre of Seats in a Garden of Dreams" lasted nearly one hour, was directed and scripted by David, and starred Roy Hudd, Ena Baga, Douglas Reeve and John Stewart. The Press Show, to which we were all invited, took place at the National Film Theatre on 17th October. Nigel Andrews, Financial Times, said 'The best passages are . . . Ena Baga recounting and demonstrating the skills of the cinema organists; the chief engineer of the magnificent and still surviving State Kilburn bewailing the death of the big picture palace; best of all some loving visual tributes to the interiors of the prize movie houses of the age – the New Victoria, the Astoria Brixton, the Granada Tooting . . .'

In October, Ena took part in an edition of 'The Organist Entertains' for the BBC with classical organist Jennifer Bate at the Compton Concert Organ in Broadcasting House, Neville Meale recorded at the Granada Kingston and Jack Ferguson at the Odeon Hammersmith. Ena played a Hammond on that occasion. The programme was by that time both produced and presented by Robin Richmond.

Robin Richmond has had a varied and interesting career, if an unusual one for a musician. Born in Queen's Gate, London, and educated at Westminster School in the Abbey precincts, the first seeds of an interest in the organ were sown when he was still a pupil. However, he studied law at London University but, probably due to his great interest in music, gave up hope of passing the examinations and turned to his first love, as Assistant to Al Bollington at the Astoria Streatham. From Streatham he went to the Queen's Forest Gate and then the Ideal Lambeth, which doubled as a Wesleyan Mission Hall. Robin got the sack for using the percussions for Sunday hymn-singing, but took over from Archie Parkhouse at the Trocette Bermondsey, where the manager billed him as 'Bob Richmond', rather than Robin!

From the Wurlitzer at Bermondsey Robin went to a fine Compton designed by Reginald Foort at the Regal Canterbury, also visiting other County cinemas at Wimbledon, Golders Green and Hove. He opened the Astoria Purley in 1934, then followed Jimmy Swift at the Granada Hove, where he stayed for three years. Late in 1937 Robin introduced the Hammond electronic organ to the UK, touring with a custom-built organ until 1941 when petrol shortages and other wartime difficulties made this impracticable. Robin then went back to the cinema organ, standing in for Al Bollington at the Paramount/Odeon Tottenham Court Road.

After the war he resumed touring the halls with his super-white Hammond, and I vividly remember his topping the bill at the Croydon Empire with Peter Brough and Archie Andrews, and his early TV appearances (in black and white!) in the Fred Emney Show. From that it was but a short step to producing for BBC Radio (e.g. 'Housewives' Choice') and of course his baby, which he first presented in 1968, 'The Organist Entertains'. His name is a house-hold one, and he is also remembered for appearances in 'Variety Bandbox', 'ITMA', 'Palace of Varieties', 'Navy Mixture', 'Shipmates Ashore', and on TV in 'Picture Parade' and in his own show, 'Organ-Grinder's Swing'.

Robin's organ-playing has always been characterized by accuracy and an attractive jazzy style. His forthright opinions, coloured by a great sense of humour were something to look forward to at lunchtime in the BBC Club 'Salad Bar' in The Langham when we were BBC colleagues in the sixties and seventies. Although Robin and his French wife, Renée, settled for a long time in the South of France, in 1992 they are back in England and we have occasionally seen the familiar shock of white hair with matching moustache compèring at Worthing Assembly Hall and the South Bank University.

At the end of October, Ena took part with David Shepherd in a concert for the Cinema Organ Society at Finchley Methodist Church. The organ at Finchley was not the usual church instrument but a Compton theatre organ, formerly in the Regal, Ilford, removed to the church under the patronage of the Minister, Reverend Leonard Barnett, a delightfully broad-minded and worldly man, who we suspect was a theatre organ enthusiast. The voicing of the organ was somewhat 'straightened' at the church for liturgical use, with the addition of strings, clarinet, open diapason and bourdon on the pedal, and a three-rank mixture to the original tibia, tuba muted trumpet, open diapason, flute and viola. The organ had been re-opened at Finchley only one month earlier, by Gerald Shaw from the Odeon Leicester Square and David Shepherd. Early in 1987 the organ moved yet again, and part of it was combined with two others at Portslade Town Hall in Sussex.

The November issue of BFI News, the organ of the British Film Institute, reported an interview between Florence and Carol Howard covering Florence's career, from her start in the orchestra pit at the Angel Islington just before the First World War to 'The doyenne of the NFT's music makers' from 1971'. 'It seems a pity', said Ms Howard, 'that the BFI cannot provide even a small organ for Florence de Jong to recall the days of the Mighty Wurlitzer at the New Gallery and a whole era of cinema history.'

In March, 1974, Ena played an electronic organ concert for the Bournemouth Organ Society and a theatre pipe organ concert for the Sheffield Theatre Organ Enthusiasts. The organ in the City School at Stradbroke, Sheffield, came from the Orpheum Golders Green, where it was once played by such well-known names as Lewis Gerard, Douglas Reeve and Reginald New. Unhappily, it was destroyed by fire in March 1990 but the STOE have obtained a replacement, originally in the Astoria Purley.

Also in March, the Mermaid Theatre, founded by Sir Bernard Miles at Puddledock, Blackfriars, presented a four-weeks Comedy Film Season with everything from the Marx Brothers and 'Ninotchka' to the 'Smallest Show on Earth' and 'High Society'. Preludes at a Rodgers 'theatre' organ had an equally impressive schedule of players including Robin Richmond, Ena Baga and Florence de Jong.

In April, Ena took part in a TV recording of 'Upstairs, Downstairs' at the Electric Cinema Portobello Road for London Weekend Television. Attired in a ginger wig, she accompanied a silent film on an upright piano, playing 'Un Peu d'Amour' as the hero, a valet, proposed to a housemaid. The rehearsal was somewhat extended, and the cast were served lunch in a double-deck bus parked nearby. Not to be outdone, Florence appeared on TV's 'Clapperboard', talking to Chris Kelly and accompanying a scene from 'College' with Buster Keaton. Richard

Afton in the Evening News was scathing about the direction: 'We saw some excerpts from really great silents from the past which were extremely interesting and which Miss de Jong accompanied on the piano and very efficiently too. But for some odd reason, while we were watching the films, every minute or so the director cut to a close up of the pianist's hands. For Pete's sake why? We all knew she was playing the piano and we presumed she was playing with her hands.'

The Daily Mail also jumped on the great silent film revival band-waggon, head-lining '. . . where would Rudolph and Buster have been without Miss Florence?' 'Rudolph Valentino, the legendary silent screen star had many glamorous partners during his career. One he never met is today still helping to perpetuate the myth of that great screen lover.' And 1974 ended with Ena is concert at the Queens Theatre, Burslem, Stoke-on-Trent. With television super chef Tony Stoppani aptly entitled 'Music and the food of love' and at Southampton Guildhall at the magnificent dual-purpose Compton. A very busy year for both ladies; not bad, when one realises that Florence was nearly eighty and Ena was approaching seventy!

CHAPTER THIRTEEN

1975 began with a letter to Ena from Charlie Chester, expressing his pleasure that she shared the nostalgia he liked to include in his radio programme. A letter from Ena had given Charlie great joy, he said, and he was going to 'cull the archives' for a recording of hers.

Having enjoyed a large measure of success with 'An Acre of Seats in a Garden of Dreams', David Furnham was now looking for another subject. Ena suggested to him that the old custom at one time prevalent in the East End of London of eel pie and mash, now dying out, would make an interesting film. And so, in 1975, David produced scripted and directed 'Noted Eel and Pie Houses', with background music by Ena and narration by the eel and pie men themselves and John Allin. 'The film records the historical development of the eel and pie houses of London from the time when eels were first brought to London by the Dutch and when pies were sold by street traders.' The film then tells the story of the eel and pie families who opened shops around the turn of the Century, such as the Cookes, the Nathans and the Harringtons, who bought their eels live from Lovat Lane, Billingsgate. 'The customers are seen through the traders' eyes and this gives a wider view of London life, reinforced by the paintings of John Allin and the music of Ena Baga.'

During the making of the film, Ena was taken with the crew to the fish-market at Leigh-on-Sea, and, at Sheekey's, in St. Martin's Lane, Florence and Ena were filmed eating eel pie and mash. For the Press Show at the National Film Theatre, the Cooke family, who started at London Fields in 1900 and with a second shop at Kingsland, Dalston, all arrived in a large Jaguar. The film was shown as part of the 19th London Film Festival at the National Film Theatre.

1976 began with an important event for Ena. On January 16th, she appeared on television with Oscar Peterson. Interviewed by Oscar, she then played solo and, on taking her bow, said 'Oscar, they've got a little piece for you.' They then both accompanied a silent film in turn, each seated at eight feet long grand pianos. Afterwards, in the Green Room, she met Count Basie, who said 'You were wonderful'.

Ten days later, Ena played in concert for the COS at the Odeon Twickenham. Her programme at the effective little six-rank Compton included music by Grieg, Kreisler, Gershwin and Friedman (Slavonic Rhapsody). Did her signature tune, 'Smoke Gets In Your Eyes', invoke memories of that fateful morning when Ena averted panic by continuing to play when a small fire broke out on stage?

At the end of March the Isle of Wight was the venue for 'The Ena Baga Weekend'. This began on the Saturday afternoon with a personal appearance at Teagues new music shop in Newport High Street, opened by Cliff Michelmore. In the evening, Islanders were invited to dine and relax for 'The Sound of Music' at the Holmwood Hotel, Cowes. On Sunday, afternoon Ena was in concert at the Apollo Theatre, Newport, for the Isle of Wight Electronic Organ Society.

In August, the 'Weekender' issued with the Southend Evening Echo, went to town with half a page devoted to 'Florence – voice of the great Valentino', marking

Ena with Oscar Peterson on Television, when they both accompanied a silent film.

a visit by both Ena and Florence to Southend to celebrate the birthday of Norah Mingay, their friend since Ena's schooldays. 'She gave Valentino a voice and cued Buster Keaton's comedy', reported Robert White. 'Today Florence de Jong is herself a star of the silent cinema . . . Tomorrow she will forget her arthritis and thump a piano at the Academy One in Oxford Street as the audience creases with laughter at the deadpan comic Buster Keaton in 'The Navigator' . . . Yesterday listeners to Radio 2's 'Open House' heard her talking about her life and music to Pete Murray.' And all that just after she celebrated her eightieth birthday!

Ena was still teaching and demonstrating on a part-time basis for Chappell's, and a visitor early in 1977 was Semprini, who chatted to her and recalled a duet they had played together on piano and organ at the Gaumont Camden Town.

In February, Beatrice's only son, clarinetist and saxophonist, Harold Palle died.

On May 29th, the Odeon Leicester Square, the Oscar Deutsch (later Rank) Flagship opened in 1937, celebrated its Silver Jubilee with a galaxy of six performers in 'Theatre Organists on Parade', organised by Bert Bartram. The ladies were represented by Ena Baga and Doreen Chadwick; and the gentlemen were Eric Spruce, former resident at the Empire over the road; Bobby Pagan, celebrating his seventieth birthday; Ray Baines, who, like Florence and Ena, spent some years back and forth across the Atlantic for Cunard; and Don Knights, former Granada and ABC organist. A special commemorative programme was produced, and the occasion was a very happy one. Ena and I were delighted to renew acquaintance with Eric Spruce and Ray Baines, both of whom had the drinks lined up at the hostelry on the corner almost before we could get there!

Theatre organ concerts followed at the Granada Kingston in July, and at Malvern Link in September. The organ at Malvern is unique for more than one reason. Having been removed from the Odeon Kingston in 1967, it was installed by Arthur Russell in Worcester – above his funeral parlour! On a very hot day in the late sixties, Ena appeared there and must have lost pounds in weight as the console had an illuminated surround in what Compton described as the 'cascade' style, complete with a hot seat! Halfway through the show, Ena turned around to the audience, fanning herself furiously and asking if anyone would like a hamburger!!

In 1971 the organ was moved to a specially built private theatre in Arthur Russell's garden at Malvern Link, and the tuba, oboe/trumpet, vox humana (so decribed because it is supposed to resemble the human voice – some are more like bleating sheep!), open diapason, tibia, flute and 'cello were supplemented by some ranks manufactured by the local organ building firm of Nicholson.

On December 18th, the Gaumont State Kilburn celebrated its 40th Anniversary with a show built around the organ, jointly arranged by the Manager, William Weir, and The Cinema Organ Society. The State had opened in December 1937 and claimed to be the largest theatre in Europe, which it wasn't; but it was the largest in England, seating just over 4,000. In the Italian Renaissance style, architecturally and decoratively as well as in its technical perfection, it reflected great credit on the architect, George Coles, who had also been responsible for such greats as the Commodore Hammersmith, Trocadero Elephant & Castle, Broadway Stratford E, Rivoli Whitchapel and about 20 Odeons of which Muswell Hill, Ipswich, Halifax and Erith were quite outstanding.

The Gaumont State had opened with great flourish, preceded by open days for public inspection filmed by Gaumont-British News, and on the night with a lavish stage show starring Gracie Fields, Vic Oliver, George Formby, Van Dam & His Orchestra and, of course, Sidney Torch at the Mighty Wurlitzer. The 40th Celebration could not quite hope to compete with that, but the Grand Anniversary show began at 11 in the morning and, with a break for lunch, continued until the beginning of the afternoon film performance at about 5 o'clock. The morning half featured at the Wurlitzer John Stewart, George Huber, Douglas Badham (Chairman of the COS) and the morning's star guest, Ena Baga.

After lunch, we opened with the Gaumont-British Newsreel of the Gaumont State including an appearance of Torch at the Wurlitzer; a line-up of stars on stage including Dame Anna Neagle, The Beverley Sisters (two of them, as one had the 'flu); Chili Bouchier and Billy Milton; followed by memories of films at the New Gallery presented by Florence de Jong; a vocal selection from 'Gigi' by the Hornsey Operatic & Dramatic Society (who regularly put on their musicals at the State); and, topping the bill, the COS President, Hubert Selby. All went like clockwork, except a nasty moment for the Host (myself) when the orchestra-lift refused to come up with the Hornsey Operatic & Dramatic and their pianist.

In May, 1978, Ena made a return visit to the Isle of Wight for a concert at the Walker organ in Ryde Town Hall. 'An Evening with Ena Baga' was arranged by the Abbeyfield Society (Bembridge Branch), and took the form of music with wine and cheese.

In October, Ena ended her part-time engagement at Chappell's. As a mark of

'Mr Wurlitzer' meets the ladies! Ena with Cathie Haigh and Ernest Broadbent (successor to Reginald Dixon at the Tower Ballroom) demonstrating for the Kimball Organ Co at the South Shore Casino in 1974. (photo: Camera & Organ Centre (Blackpool), John Nunns & Stephen Austin).

their appreciation for the valuable contribution she had made and all she had done for the company over the years, Ronnie Falk invited her to dinner with ten of Chappell's executives at the Old Vienna Restaurant in Bond Street. Was she serenaded with Viennese Memories of Lehar, I wonder?

'Viennese Memories of Lehar' was the title of one of many 78rpm records of Al Bollington, during his residency at the Paramount, later Odeon, Tottenham Court Road. Al began his musical career at the age of eighteen when he ran away to sea as ship's pianist. In 1925, he was playing a 2-manual Mustel organ, pumped by pedals, at the Palace Blackpool. In 1928, but for the fact that he had accepted a post at the Grange Cinema Kilburn, he might well have become the Blackpool Tower Ballroom organist instead of his friend and golfing partner, Reginald Dixon! In 1929 Al went to the newly-opened and incredible atmospheric cinema, the Astoria Brixton; in 1931 he opened a similar Compton organ with twin consoles at the Streatham Astoria, with, as his assistant, a young Robin Richmond. The London Astorias were quickly taken over by British Paramount and they posted Al to their London Showcase, the Plaza Piccadilly in 1935, in succession to Charles Smart.

A year later, Paramount opened their new theatre in Tottenham Road with Reginald Foort at a fine Compton, and after a short while Al succeeded him. Through broadcasts and recordings, many with Anton and the Paramount Theatre Orchestra, Al became well known and he remained at the Paramount/Odeon until 1948 (apart from distinguished service in the RAF when his deputies at the

102

Paramount were Molly Forbes, followed by Robin Richmond). Al left to open an organ at the new Odeon/Carlton Toronto, never to return, and Britain's loss was a gain for Canada and later the USA. Al corresponded with Ena during 1979, from California, recalling her 'excellent technique and styling' in BBC broadcasts. He sent Ena a copy of his composition 'Hoe Down' which she later broadcast. Al mentioned that he had been invited to come over and perform concerts at the Odeons at Leicester Square and Birmingham (former Paramount, which he opened in 1937) but he had undergone surgery to his left hand and was doubtful if he could play well enough. In the event, he did not return to England, which is a pity. Al died in November 1991 in a Los Angeles nursing home, but we do have memories of him on record, not least of which is 'Viennnese Memories of Lehar', which was chosen by Robin Richmond and myself for inclusion in the BBC's Golden Jubilee theatre organ LP issued in 1972. Of all the records issued to commemorate the Jubilee, the theatre organ album proved to be a best-seller!

In October 1979, Ena made another TV appearance, miming piano playing in 'Kate The Good Neighbour', and the following month she was 'guest organist' of the week on BBC Radio Medway which broadcast extracts from 'Sounds of the Music of Richard Rodgers', prompting a response from several listeners. A further TV appearance took place in the following February, when, dressed as a pub pianist with an old-fashioned hat, Ena was seen and heard in 'All Creatures Great and Small'.

In July, 1980, The American Theatre Organ Society celebrated their Silver Jubilee with a Convention in London. On the fourth day, the Wednesday, they took tea at Clayhall, Ilford, followed by a concert on the beautiful Compton theatre organ in the St John Vianney Church by Ena Baga. The organ, originally installed in the Ritz Cinema Nuneaton, is a cracker and has been further enhanced by the magnificient acoustic properties of this modern Roman Catholic Church.

At the end of November, The Cinema Organ Society presented both Florence and Ena in concert at the sweet little Model 'F' Wurlitzer, where they had both been resident more than fifty years previously. Florence's programme took the form of reminscences of the New Gallery from Opening Night in 1925 through to 1937, while Ena's contribution included Frederick Curzon's delightful 'March of the Bowmen', a salute to British Winter Weather with tunes about fog, rain and snow, and the Farandole from Bizet's 'L'Arlesienne Suite No. 2'. In the second half, both ladies entertained with an organ and piano duet in a varied programme ranging from the Litolff 'Scherzo' to Zez Confrey's 'Dizzy Fingers' and fairly brought the house down.

A high spot occurred for Ena in the Summer of 1981 when she was contracted by Film International of Rotterdam to record the accompaniment to 15 programmes of silent comedies at the Standaart theatre organ at the Passage Theatre, Schiedam, Holland. Each programme lasted just over an hour, and Ena spent five days at the theatre. This must have been very hard work for a lady not in her first flush of youth, but such was her reputation for silent film accompaniment that no-one else would suffice! The Passage is almost unique in that it is a live theatre containing a cinema organ. Films are occasionally shown with organ accompaniment but the Passage has never been a full-time cinema. After several days of concentrated work at the theatre with Laurel & Hardy and Charlie Chaplin, etc., Ena was taken to Kinderdyke, which has 20 windmills. During the Second World War, the slats of the windmills were left in certain positions as a code for allied aircraft. After this little expedition and an afternoon off, Ena returned to the theatre until the Friday to complete the recording. On the Saturday she was taken to Amsterdam for a boat trip on the canals and to play the Wurlitzer/Strunk organ at the Tuschinski Theatre. I visited the Tuschinski when on holiday in Amsterdam, and the organ is an absolute beauty! Not to mention the theatre, which has a 'listing', protecting it as a building of architectural merit.

CHAPTER FOURTEEN

For several years, both ladies had been appearing in concert at The Music Museum, in Brentford, which, in addition to the fantastic collection of automatic musical instruments amassed over the years by the late Frank Holland, has the fine Wurlitzer formerly in the Regal at Kingston-On-Thames. I have always regarded this as one of the best, Wurlitzers in the UK, and when it left the theatre in 1972 for reinstallation at the Brentford Museum, I wondered whether the distinct and glorious 'Kingston Sound' would be preserved. It was very carefully installed at Brentford, in chambers to one side of the vast church that serves as the Museum, and from the re-opening by Joseph Seal in 1973 it was obvious that the quality of the instrument was still there. In the summer of 1981 Florence and Ena performed solo and in duet on organ and grand piano as usual, but with one difference. Peter Borrowdale, who has a fine tenor voice and has trained for solo work with various London choirs, sang solos with both Florence and Ena accompanying at the Wurlitzer. The evening was very well received.

1982 was a fairly busy year, with Ena paying a second visit to Compton Lodge, Sapcote, Leicestershire, the home of Paul and Hazel Kirner and the Compton theatre organ formerly in the Odeon Wealdstone. A small instrument of only 5 ranks in one chamber, it was where a young Harold Smart first cut his teeth in 1938. It was removed to the Chandos Secondary School at Stanmore in 1961, then to the Park High School Harrow, but in 1979 re-opened, slightly enlarged, at Paul & Hazel Kirner's home by John Mann. Not many people can claim to have a home with a room large enough to stage theatre organ concerts, parties and regular dances!

In May there were three events: a concert by Ena at the Memorial Hall Old Windsor at the Compton formerly in the Regal Old Kent Road; an electronic concert at the Pony Inn on the Channel Island of Guernsey; and a visit to the Assembly Hall Worthing, where Florence, Ena and myself were the guests at the Anniversary Concert of the Sussex Theatre Organ Trust. Towards the end of summer, the ladies were spending a weekend with Jean Broad, widow of Leslie Broad of the John Compton Organ Company, at her flat in Westgate-on-Sea.

In November, Ena played a concert at the Regal Henley-on-Thames, at a Compton theatre organ opened there in 1972 by Reginald Dixon. Like the Odeon at Blackpool, the Regal Henley received a second-hand organ, in this case from the Ritz Tunbridge Wells. Four years later, the Regal suddenly closed in a blaze of publicity and under a barrage of local opposition, as the owners wished to sell it to Waitrose for a supermarket extension.

The year closed with a visit to the Compass Theatre, Ickenham, where, at the invitation of Director John Sherrat, we all took part in their Christmas show. Florence and Ena were firm favourites, and the Annual end-of-the-year event would have been incomplete without them.

1983 proved to be another year full of activity; amazing, when one considers that

A Queen and a Duchess! Ena recording at the Odeon Leicester Square Compton ('The Duchess') in 1976 for her album, 'Sounds of the Music of Richard Rodgers'.

Ena reached her 77th birthday, whereas Florence was now 86! Three venues in Nottinghamshire were visited by Ena in March. First, the Avondale Wurlitzer at the home of Tom and Joan Bagley at Sutton-in-Ashfield. This organ was originally at the Regal Beckenham but was removed to St Dominic's Hall at Cowley, Oxford in 1964. It moved again in 1979, to Tom and Joan's home where it was installed in a specially-built Music Room.

Only a week later, we journeyed to the home of Ray and Vera Booth, who live at nearby Mansfield. Their house, Branksome, is a handsome one, and Ray built a Music Room in the orchard to house most of the Compton that he removed from the Regal Handsworth, Birmingham, in 1973. The Branksome concert was scheduled for the Sunday evening, but on the Saturday we drove to Newark and, after lunch with Charles and Dorothy McNicol, to the 'Regal Lodge' (a miniature cinema) at the home of Bryan Richardson in Newark. The organ, a Compton, came from the Savoy Cinema Lincoln and was installed at Newark in 1979. The 'Regal' has a flat floor and can be used for dancing, parties and film shows as well as concerts; silent film shows with accompaniment on both pipe and electronic organs are a regular feature. Charles McNicol, in addition to arranging the shows at Regal Lodge, is an organist in his own right and made guest appearances at the Granada Grantham in the 1950s as 'Charlie McNicol, Newark's talented organist'. He occasionally plays an evening at The Plough, Great Munden, the only pub in the world with a theatre organ.

The concerts at Branksome were always happy and most enjoyable affairs, with

Ray as compère and Vera producing a superb buffet for the interval. Sadly, in 1986 they announced that they were not getting any younger and the Branksome Compton was offered for sale, with a farewell concert by Arnold Loxam on 3 May.

At the end of March all three of us went to the State Grays for a Sunday concert, and in May to the Assembly Hall Worthing for the Anniversary Show. On May 31st both Florence and Ena recorded a complete programme for BBC Radio 2 in 'The Organist Entertains' series, taking tea with producer Peter Pilbeam and presenter Nigel Ogden. On June 6th, both attended the Annual Dinner of the Cinema and Television Veterans at the Lancaster Gate hotel.

In mid-June, Ena was due to play in concert at Southampton Guildhall, and decided to spend a few days at Bournemouth. I drove her down and we spent the weekend with kind friends, Patrick and Mary Whittet in their nice little bunglow in Lower Parkstone, near Compton Acre. I say 'little' but appearances must be deceptive as they have a large music room with organ and grand piano, and there is a billiard room. Their small triangular garden is a piece cut out of the golf-course and the cover over the swimming pool must occasionally trap the odd golf ball as well as falling leaves. Pat and Muff (she is known to her friends as 'Muff' as at one time she always went about with her hands in a fur muff) are charming hosts, and I always imagine that Muff just missed being an actress as she has such poise and elegance. I could see her in the part of the ghost of Elvira, Charles Condomine's first wife in 'Blithe Spirit'. In fact, Pat would make a first-rate Charles, with Ena as Madam Arcati!

In October Ena played the South Bank Wurlitzer for the COS, and towards the end of November we journeyed to Gunton Hall, a country club and holiday centre, near Lowestoft in Suffolk, for a concert on their Compton theatre organ in the ballroom. On the Saturday evening, we went with Terry Hepworth to Gorleston-on-Sea, to the Palace Bingo Club (former cinema), where Terry has installed a large Compton on the stage. He plays each evening during the bingo interval and the five-manual console with its gleeming rows of 'teeth' looks very impressive as the curtains open.

Later that month Ena was asked by Thames Television to take part in the (1983) 'Morecambe and Wise Christmas Show', involving rehearsals at Richmond Athletic Club and a recording at Teddington Studios on December 9th. Ena cannot remember why she was unable to fulfil this exciting engagement and Thames Television have confirmed that her place at the piano was taken by Gracie Cole, so it remains a mystery!

All Fool's Day happened to be on a Sunday in 1984, and this gave the COS the chance to stage a concert at the Granada Walthamstow with both music and merriment. The organ in the Granada (now Cannon) is a very fine Christie with two consoles, one on stage and the other on a lift in the orchestra pit. Unfortunately, the latter cannot now be used as it is hidden beneath a stage apron extension, but it was in full working order on April 1 and was put to good use in a short comedy act involving John Leeming and organ technician, John Abson. The guest organists were Ena Baga, Nigel Ogden, Carolyn Riddick and David Shepherd. At a previous concert involving both David Shepherd and Ena, David had over-run in spite of precision timing in his schedule leaving Ena, as top of the bill, less than her alloted

Looking like a queen, Ena at the Connaught Hotel in 1977 with Teddy Holmes of Chappells at his retirement party. (photo: Doug Mackenzie).

time. Ena was to follow David at Walthamstow on April 1st, so John Abson manufactured a 'lollipop' with STOP and GO on each side and the audience were highly amused to see Ena march out with STOP prominently displayed. As David concluded his part, the sign was turned to show GO, and there was more laughter. As London District Secretary, John Leeming wrote to Ena with a 'big thank you' for her contribution to the show. 'I have been approached by a great many people at various events since that day', says John, 'all of whom have said how much they enjoyed the music and the spirit of fun and good humour at the concert.'

On Monday, 11th June, the Conservatives held a Rally for Europe at the Central Hall Westminter, preceded by 45 minutes of popular organ music played by Ena Baga, culminating in a 'Song for Europe'. The Rally concluded with an address by the, then, Prime Minister, Margaret Thatcher, who personally thanked Ena for her organ music and asked for 'three cheers for the organist'. A proud day for Ena indeed!

O.K. for Silents! Florence was appointed Musical Director to the National Film Theatre in 1971.

CHAPTER 15

On January 13th, Ena played in concert at the Odeon, Birmingham, which had a good Compton opened by her old friend Al Bollington in 1937. It was the only organ left in a former Paramount, and Ena had top billing with Ken Stroud, Iain Flitcroft, Dorian Collins, Steve Tovey (who at that time was playing the Compton regularly) and Mike Slater from Blackpool. Ken Stroud is a seasoned entertainer, having started his career at the age of 14 as a 'Wonder Boy Organist' at the Globe Cinema Clapham Junction. He had various short appointments at York, Potters Bar, Slough and with Granada before his war service, returning to civilian life as resident organist at the Ritz Nuneaton and its beautiful Compton. He left the cinema world in 1948 and freelanced, taking over from the great Jerry Allen as organist to Jan Ralfini and His Orchestra and eventually becoming Musical Director and Company Organist to Zetters Leisure. As well as a fine musician, Ken is a genial person and is an ideal musical host for any party, as exemplified at Ramsgate for the 40th Birthday of (young) David Willis. Ken and his charming wife, Beryl, still live in Nuneaton, where they are well-known.

On February 20th, the Southend Evening Echo went to town with a headline 'Ena brings back her magic', alongside a very nice picture of Ena and Florence at a grand piano. 'Long, long ago when today's great grandmas were young, a Southend schoolgirl used to fit music to the mood of silent movies. Little Ena Baga wove the magic on the organ at the Strand Cinema, long since demolished to make way for an extension to Keddie's Southend store. She played for the children's Saturday picture show as they sat on the edge of their seats munching their free issue of a bag of sweets and an apple. Incredibly, more than 65 years later, Ena is still creating the mood for cinema buffs at the National Film Theatre on the South Bank with her older and equally well-known sister, Florence de Jong . . .'

The article went on to detail Ena's career, and was in connection with her visit three days later to Rochford Hospital to play the Compton theatre organ in the recreation hall. The organ had begun its life in 1936 at the nearby Kingsway Cinema Hadleigh, and had been re-opened at Rochford in April 1984 by Peggy Weber, who, at the age of 18, had opened it in its original home at Hadleigh. Peggy, today living in retirement in a little cottage near Ashford, Kent, told us a marvellous story about the opening night way back in 1936. Her tutor, the great George Thalben-Ball, went down to Hadleigh for the opening night and volunteered to play the National Anthem for her. Groping for the drum-roll toe piston, he accidentally hit the klaxon, and although this was hardly noticed by the audience, it had both 'G. T-B.' and Peggy in fits of laughter for the rest of the evening.

During March, Ena accompanied a Buster Keaton silent at the Compass Theatre Ickenham, played a concert at the Southampton Guildhall, and appeared for the COS at Marston Green Hospital at another Compton installed in a hospital recreation hall. This organ had its origin at the Tower Cinema West Bromwich and

'Smoke Gets in Your Eyes' – nearly! Florence and Ena hosting a luncheon at the National Film Theatre for Michael Bentine and the 'Quick on the Draw' TV crew. To the immediate right of Ena is Leslie Hardcastle, NFT Director.

had been re-opened at Marston Green Maternity Hospital in 1971 by the COS Founder, Hubert Selby and the Matron, who, brandishing a large pair of scissors, announced that she was going to cut the organ's umbilical cord! A good job she didn't, as we should have had no sound that afternoon. The recreation hall became needed for other things, and the organ was removed to storage for a while, before being rebuilt and re-opened at St Martin's School, Solihull, on April 4th 1992 by COS Chairman David Shepherd and Simon Gledhill.

At this time the COS was arranging concerts at the Blackpool Tower Ballroom, and that for May 12th 1985 featured Ena Baga as the guest of resident organist Phil Kelsall. This was Ena's first apparance at the Tower Wurlitzer for 40 years, and she was greatly looking forward to it. Ena was escorted to Blackpool by Southend organist, Victor Patterson. They had to change trains three times, and Ena described the journey as a 'Rail Fiasco'. However, the concert went off well, and for Ena it must have been an emotional experience to return to the scene of her great triumph during the war years.

At the end of May, busy Ena went down to Poole to stay with friends John and Beryl Chalmers, visiting the Isle of Wight for a party with her great friend Ron Jackson, and on the Sunday appearing at Sandford Park as special guest organist.

August 7th was my birthday, and I decided to have a special party at The Plough, Great Munden, with 12 guests including Ena as Guest of Honour. Margaret and Tony Merridale, hosts and owners of The Plough (they bought the pub because

112

they wanted the theatre organ) regard Ena as their favourite organist, and everything was splendidly arranged for my little party, which I had in the Compton Lounge with the organ, which was removed from the Gaumont Finchley to The Plough in 1967. Both Ena and Victor Patterson played during the evening, and we all had a good time. It was a good thing that the 7th fell on a Wednesday as The Plough is busy at weekends, with guest organists on Friday, Saturday and Sunday evenings. What nicer way for organ enthusiasts to spend a few hours, especially as there is a full menu and The Plough is in a remote spot in beautiful Hertfordshire countryside – delightful in spring and summer! Remember to book a table, though!

A month later Florence and Ena were in concert at The Music Museum at the Wurlitzer, and in duet at the organ and grand piano. Florence had a bad back, and I had to stand behind her at rehearsal and rub her back the entire time. Oddly, it disappeared for the actual concert. At the conclusion, turning to the audience, Ena said 'Wish Us Luck As You Wave Us Good-bye'; and then shouted 'in F!' to Florence at the piano which had the entire front row in fits of laughter.

At the end of September we were again at Rochford Hospital, dining with Victor and Ruby Patterson at their Rayleigh home; and at the end of October Ena played yet another Compton, this time at the Napton Nickelodeon, a musical museum cleverly constructed in a redundant Methodist Chapel. Graham and Pat Whitehead were hosts, and Graham had devised a museum with all the mechanical exhibits and the console of the Compton at ground floor level, but with a cinema/theatre at first-floor level, with projection box at the rear, small stage and

Taking time off from recording music for silents in Holland, 1981. (photo: Fjitte De Vries, Rotterdam).

Ena tickles the ivories as the village pub pianist in 'All Creatures Great and Small' – March 1980. (photo: Neil Wigley, Birmingham).

All Fools' Day at the Granada Walthamstow. Ena in concert for the COS at the Christie theatre organ, with Nigel Ogden, David Shepherd, Carolyn Riddick and flautist, Timothy Cousin (April 1, 1984). (photo: John D. Sharp).

'orchestra pit', through which the console rose on a scissors lift from the ground floor below. Ingenious.

Graham and Pat acquired so many exhibits that the small theatre began to burst at the seems, and in 1990 the whole museum was moved to Ashorne Hall, south of Leamington Spa, and reinstalled in a purpose-built theatre attached to the Hall in beautiful surroundings. The ceiling of the theatre came from the County Cinema Warwick; small ventilation grilles from the Regal Atherstone; and the grilles for the organ chambers, the main chandelier and balustrade from the Granada Bedford. So, the theatre has a real atmosphere. Ken Stroud, Rachael Ward and Craig Boswell re-opened the Compton, and I re-opened the museum, in July 1991.

Perhaps the main event for Ena and Florence during 1985 was the Mobil British Film Institute Awards ceremony, at the National Film Theatre on June 25th. The ceremony, to celebrate outstanding achievement by people in the film industry, was hosted by Richard Attenborough before an audience of 450 celebrities from stage and screen, including Dame Anna Neagle, Sir Douglas Fairbanks Junior, Peter Cushing, Joan Bakewell and Anthony Andrews. The BFI Book Award was won by Richard Schickel, principal film critic of, Time magazine (for 'D. W. Griffith and the Birth of the Film'); and was presented to him by Florence de Jong and Ena Baga. 'Mobil News' paid tribute to the two ladies, stating that between them they had 128 years experience of working in the film industry as pianists and organists.

115

'During their careers they have provided musical accompaniment to many silent films and have played for all the great silent stars.'

Early in November I took Ena to The Plough for one of her Saturday evening performances there, and it was nice that we were joined by a party from Coventry headed by our great friend Dorothy Marcus, a live wire in the local organ society and a hospitable lady who has provided comfortable beds and good food on more than one occasion.

The last week or two of the year were not comfortable ones for Ena as she had to go into hospital for an operation. That amazingly plucky lady agreed to play a concert at the Odeon Leicester Square (for Bert Bartram) on December 15th, the day she entered hospital. From her performance, no-one would have known that she was about to undergo major surgery, and the show was a great success. Florence and I were among the audience, and afterwards the two ladies met Ron Jackson from the Isle of Wight for lunch.

Ena had her operation on December 17th. On the following day, her first visitors were Florence and myself, and, in her own words, Ena felt 'like Hell'. Nevertheless, she was sitting up in bed, belching defiantly at the world and protesting that she couldn't help it! Two days later, Ena was feeling better but was still only taking water. Florence poked about in the bedside locker, looking for a bottle of Scotch that Ena could not of course make any use of. Suddenly, Ena's patience snapped

The old folks at home! Ena and Florence return to Southend-on-Sea for a concert in 1984.

116

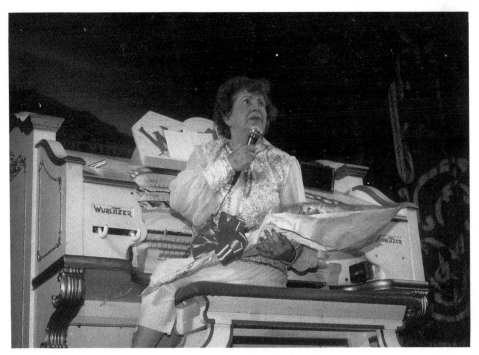

Together again after 40 years! Ena returns to the Tower Blackpool in 1985, and the management says it with flowers.

and she said 'Florence, stop poking about – you're getting on my nerves!' 'Don't you talk to me like that!', retorted Florence, and then showed how kind she was by walking as steadily around the ward as her arthritis would allow, watering all the plants!

A week after the operation, Ena was allowed tea and fruit drinks but still no food, and on Christmas Eve she had a further operation. All was successful, and, having spent Christmas in hospital, she went to St Leonards to convalesce. St Leonards is very pleasant in summer but in winter it looks somewhat abandoned, and the first few days of Ena's convalescence were very cold and wet. Some flowers from the National Film Theatre brightened her outlook, followed by a visit by Floence and myself. Ena returned home after two weeks, and on the following day she was almost her old self when we celebrated her 80th birthday at a restaurant next-door to the Kensington Odeon, with Florence and Ena's very kind friends from Twickenham, Bill and Joan Hiscock. They had ferried Ena to and from St Leonards, and there was nothing they would not do for her. Brian Parsons, Manager of the Odeon, grabbed ten minutes off from his busy theatre to bring in a bottle of champagne, and it was quite a night!

On St Valentine's Day, February 14th, the COS staged a special concert on their magnificent Wurlitzer at the South Bank Polytechnic, starring the 'Wurlitzer Wizard' from the Blackpool Tower, Phil Kelsall. Ena was Guest of Honour, making her first public appearance since the Odeon concert in mid-December, and she was presented with a large bouquet of flowers.

The events of the weekend 11/13 April 1986 as they affected Ena were one of the all-time best kept of secrets. I had told Ena that she would be asked to accompany some silent comedies at Gunton Hall during the annual Organ Weekend but that this would not be announced as she was to be a surprise guest. She kept asking why she had no contract and which films she would be playing for. In the end, I arranged with the Director of Gunton Hall for a contract to be sent, and I said that the films were all short comedies that she knew. This seemed to satisfy Ena, and on Friday 11th I drove her to Gunton Hall. She understood that she should be kept out of the way, and was put up at the Cliff Hotel, Gorleston-on-Sea for the night.

On the Saturday Ena was collected from the hotel for the main evening event (supposedly her accompaniment of silents) and, as I was dressed to go on stage, I kept out of the way behind a pillar when she was conducted onto the stage. Ena was introduced by Terry Hepworth, noticing as she went on stage that the screen was in a funny position in relation to the grand piano. At a suitable point during Terry's opening words, I interrupted with a red book in the style of the TV series and announced to an astonished Ena and a wildly enthusiastic audience that we were going to tell her life story. Having got over the shock and surprise, Ena thoroughly enjoyed herself, meeting her old school-chum, Norah Mingay from Southend (who had been kept comfortably out of the way all day), and a host of people who had played a part in her life, such as Presenter of BBC Radio 2 'The Organist Entertains', Nigel Ogden; William Davies; Douglas Reeve (recorded message); pupil Victor Patterson; David Shepherd, and the lady who followed her at Lyons' Oxford St. Corner House in 1951, Doreen Chadwick, who appeared in a wonderful reproduction of a Lyons' 'nippy' outfit made by the Director's wife and who served Ena with a welcome gin and tonic! All in all, a successful evening, and many friends said that it was the highlight of the weekend.

On the Sunday, Ena was invited to join the panel to select The Cinema Organ Society's Young Theatre Organist of the Year.

CHAPTER SIXTEEN

On May 25th, 1986, Ena and myself were guests at the Anniversary V Show at Worthing Assembly Hall. It was a show to remember, with star American organists Walt Strony and Carlo Curley topping the bill, Carlo giving the Allen touring Digital Computer Organ its first public airing. Bandleader Ken Mackintosh performed saxophone solos with organ accompaniment; and the biggest surprise was when compère Nigel Ogden introduced Ernest Broadbent, making a return to the Wurlitzer, and the sight and sound of Ernest rising out of the pit to the strains of the signature tune heard for so many years at the Tower Ballroom, 'For You', brought tears to many eyes. Walt and Carlo's Grand Finale was a duet on pipes and computer organ of the famous Toccata from Widor's Fifth Symphony that brought the house down! After the show Ena and I dined with Rita and Jean Walter, who have a charming 'Retirement retreat' at West Worthing.

Florence had not been too well during 1986, and in June spent a short spell in St Stephen's Hospital, Fulham Road, where Ena and I visited her. Florence kept repeating how wonderful it was that we had gone such a long way to see her. So often, in fact, that Ena was moved to say 'Well, it's not as if we came all the way from Mars!'

In July, Ena gave a concert at Ventor, in the basement of a jeweller's shop, where Peter Bottomley and Clive Hemming had installed a Compton, originally from the Pavilion Reading but via Rayleigh Parish Church in Essex and a restaurant in Worcester, and much altered en route! Unfortunately, Peter was ill in hospital and Clive was visiting him, so I was pressed into compèring the show. Sadly, Peter died at the end of July. He was well-known and respected locally, and Holy Trinity, Ventnor, was packed for his funeral service, including the Mayor of Ventnor. Michael Wooldridge of Portslade played for the service.

On August 1st Florence reached her 90th birthday. Having just come out of hospital the day before, she was a little tired but full of life and sipped a little whiskey as friends gathered around her at her Kensington Church Street flat to wish her 'Happy Birthday'. The piano was stacked high with cards and the fireplace looked like a flower boutique. Ena, with the help of Joan and Bill Hiscock, organised the tea and Yvonne Smith brought a beautiful birthday cake with nine candles. The telephone hardly stopped ringing, but, when it did, Ena entertained at the piano. A superb bouquet of flowers was delivered from the Ashford Manor Golf Club, both ladies having been members there for years. Friend Norah from Southend, together with Lilian and Gina Langsfield, Joe Shaw and George Muteau all joined us during the course of the afternoon. Bill, Joan and I did the washing-up!

A few days later, I drove Ena down to Crowborough to spend the day with John and Mavis Sharp. John's father was head gardener at Titsey Park, in Surrey, but John did not follow in father's muddy foot-steps. No, he developed an interest in the organ at an early age, and by the late thirties had become a theatre organist on the Granada circuit. He had some photographs taken of himself at the console but

119

Ladies only! Ena at Epsom Playhouse in concert with Janet Dowsett, Doreen Chadwick and Julie-Anne Carr, October 1986.

as not particularly impressed with them and, after his wartime service during which he met and married Mavis in South Africa, he decided that he could do a better job than the photographer had done and became a professional. His photographs are well-known throughout the organ world, and since his retirement to Sussex he has become involved in the Tunbridge Wells & Erith Railway Preservation Society (TWERPS), the David Solomons Society and local history, about which he gives talks. The David Solomons Society are concerned with the restoration of the Welte organ in the Engineering Theatre in David Salomons House, and John has been very active in helping with their fund-raising.

In all these activities, John's late wife, Mavis, was a tower of strength, particularly in the secretarial and administrative work connected with John's photographic and railway interests. She loved Ena, and was always so hospitable, insisting that I take Ena down to lunch and tea several times a year. It was a very sad day for all of us when Mavis died after a long illness, but John has borne it all very bravely and keeps busy, looking forward to visits from people like 'young Ena'.

From late July until late August, a series of programmes in which both Ena and I took part called 'A Splendid Discipline' was transmitted on BBC Radio 4. Directed by Manchester Popular Music Producer, Peter Pilbeam, and presented by Diane Shelley, the series traced the development of music in the cinema, from early day pianos through the orchestras to the cinema organ and the advent of 'talkies'.

Early in September, Ena appeared with three other lady organists at the new

120

Epsom Playhouse. Supporting Ena on the bill were Doreen Chadwick, Julie-Anne Carr and Janet Dowsett, the organ(s) of course being electronic there being no theatre organ at Epsom. Although it had five cinemas at different times including a lovely Capitol, Epsom never did have a theatre organ.

In November, Ena was approached by Skyline Film and Television for a package item, including interview and a performance of one of her own compositions.

Florence was now a little frail and had returned to hospital after a fall in her flat. It was decided that she should not be left alone, and she went to live in a rest home for the elderly in Wimbledon. The Matron was a jolly Irish lady, and Florence was well looked-after, even having an electronic organ in her room! Ena and I were of course regular visitors, and we never failed to have a singsong around the organ. At Christmas time we involved all the other residents, and Mrs. Curly brought in a tray of drinks!

One more event before 1986 came to a close was a return to the Granada Walthamstow, featuring Ena with teacher-and-pupil team Stephen Vincent and Paul Sheffield. Both Stephen and Paul had previously qualified as ATOS (London) Young Organists of the Year.

Popular organist and all-round entertainer John Mann was the first Artistic Director to the annual Fairfield Organ Festival, staged each January at the Fairfield Halls, Croydon, when the complex is open all day from 10 o'clock and there is something happening all day long. The 1987 Festival was held on January 20th, and for something completely different Ena Baga accompanied silent comedy classics in the main concert hall. Ena was also interviewed on the art of silent film accompanient, at which she must be the UK's greatest expert, by compère Nigel Ogden. At lunchtime there was the customery 'Jazz at the Fairfield' with Harry Stoneham, followed in the afternoon by a classical spectacular and International popular organ entertainment in the evening. There are demonstrations, tuition and display stands all day long, and there is always a tremendous atmosphere in the Fairfield on this day.

Always in demand for film accompaniment, Ena played to the Lon Chaney film 'Phantom of the Opera' at the Compass Theatre in March and for other films at the National Film Theatre in April and May. In June, she performed the same funtion at Greenwich, close to Old Father Thames, when the Trident Hall presented 'An Evening of Old Movies with Ena Baga'.

Returning to the theatre pipe organ, she was in concert with Doreen Chadwick at the mighty five-manual Compton at the Odeon Leicester Square on June 7th and at The Plough Great Munden for the 50th Anniversary Show on July 20th.

If the structure of the Gaumont Finchley had remained intact for just a few further months, it would have reached its 50th Anniversary. The Compton, however, celebrated its Golden Jubilee on July 20th in its second home, The Plough Great Munden, where it had been well cared for for twenty years. Tony and Margaret Merridale staged a 50th Anniversary Celebration featuring Ena, with George Blackmore and David Shepherd, and myself as compère. We had a superb evening, with a buffet included in the seat price, as well as a marvellous souvenir programme on the lines of the original opening programme for the Gaumont Finchley. A night to remember!

In August there were three further silent film evenings at the National Film Theatre, and at the end of the month we spent a week on the Isle of Wight, including a return to Nunwell House, where Ena played a Yamaha organ and the second half of the programme was devoted to two silent comedy films, Laurel & Hardy in 'The Music Box' and Charlie Chaplin in 'Easy Street'. We returned on the ferry from Yarmouth to Lymington, lunching with two lovely friends of Ena's, Rosie and Tony Bradley at their home in Downton. It was a very hot day and we sat on their terrace having lunch 'al fresco', with a superb view of The Needles from the garden. Tony and Rosie decided they needed a swim, so we went to the beach at Milford-on-Sea where Ena insisted on having a paddle. The shingle proved too much for Ena's sensitive feet, and if it hadn't been for Rosie and me holding her up she would have sat in the sea!

In September there were theatre organ concerts at The Music Museum (not quite so much fun without Florence), at Southampton Guildhall and at The Plough. The COS produces a quarterly journal 'Cinema Organ' and a monthly Newsletter of 12 pages. The latter was edited by Ian Sutherland for 23 years until his untimely death in 1981, and his memory is perpetuated by an annual Ian Sutherland Award, given to a promising young organist who receives the Award in concert with an established professional. The 1987 Award went to Iain Flitcroft, who had begun his theatre organ career with two seasons at the Tower Blackpool and in the 1990s is an experienced theatre organist, specialising in strict-tempo for dancing. He appeared with Ena at the Cannon Cinema Northampton on October 4th; Ena including two silents, Laurel & Hardy in 'Keep 'Em Laughing' and Charles Chaplin in 'The New Janitor'. The organ at the Cannon is the second Compton to be installed there. As the Savoy, the cinema opened in 1936 with a Compton of 7 ranks transferred from the Princess Cinema at Dagenham. It was opened by Wilfred Southworth, who specialised in opening organs for ABC, followed co-incidentally by Joseph Flitcroft (no relation to Award-winner Iain). The last two resident organists in the 1940s and 50s were Verden Waugh (one of the famous Waugh family) and Harold Nash who was there until 1956. The second installation, also a Compton, was made up from pipework from the Ritz Cleethorpes and the Warner Leicester Square, and was opened in May 1986 by Ronald Curtis and Michael Wooldridge, with variety acts and myself as compère. Organ builder David Pawlyn was able to use the original organ chambers, and lift for the console.

The Sussex Theatre Organ Trust were in a nostalgic frame of mind in October 1987 when they presented 'Thanks for the Memory' at Worthing Asembly Hall, featuring four cinema organists from the era when they were in great demand – Ena Baga, George Blackmore, Bobby Pagan and Louis Mordish. The formula had proved highly successful at the South Bank Polytechnic six months earlier with a capacity audience, and it was good to realise that folks would turn out in force to hear the real old professionals. Ena said on the 'phone: 'He's having all the old crocks!', but I'm sure she didn't mean it!

'Old Crock' or not, Ena is well regarded, particularly in Europe, where her reputation as a silent film accompanist is second to none. In November 1987, she was invited to Switzerland, to play for silents and to appear in concert at the College Claparede, near Geneva.

'Thanks for the Memory'. The Worthing Wurlitzer is host in 1987 to four of the UK's professional theatre organists: George Blackmore, Ena, Bobby Pagan and Louis Mordish, introduced by Nigel Ogden. (photo: John D. Sharp).

The Wurlitzer at Claperede was originally installed in the Granada Clapham Junction, and opened there by Donald Thorne in 1937. The theatre, which stands proudly above Clapham Junction station and is currently a bingo club, was an 'improved' version of the Komisarjevsky Granada interiors, and is worthy of listing as a building of architectural merit but at the time of writing all attempts by the Cinema Theatre Association have been rejected. The organ is one of the second batch of eight-rank Granada Wurlitzers, with stronger strings, i.e. gamba and gamba celeste rather than violin and violin celeste, and English horn and saxophone instead of vox humana and clarinet. The placing of the organ chambers under the stage made it an outstanding and powerful organ, much to the liking of the BBC, and it is sorely missed.

The organ was removed from Clapham and taken to Geneva in 1980, purchased by Swiss Cinema Organ Society member, Jacques Jonneret. Due to various technical problems, it could not be installed in a musical museum as intended, but in the college hall, equipped with 35mm and 16mm projectors. The inaugural concert was given at Claperede by our old friend, Robin Richmond, then living in France. Ena found the Wurlitzer to be in good condition, and it sounded well in the large College concert hall. She played to Buster Keaton's 'Steamboat Bill', one of his best, she said, and a very good copy. She gave a short concert before the film, and managed to greet the audience in her 'best French', telling them that she spoke the language like a 'French cow', which raised a loud laugh.

Ena's recital included some French tunes and melodies of Fats Waller, etc., particularly enjoyed by some Americans in the audience. The film, with organ accompaniment, was well received, and a party for Ena was given afterwards at the hotel. The Keaton film was repeated for the students on the following day, and Ena says that they enjoyed it immensely, which is good because they will be the audiences of the future. Ena stayed on for a few days, hosted by one of the tutors, who had a delightful house by the side of Lac Leman (Lake of Geneva), and she spent the time lunching and shopping, not in Geneva but over the border in northern France where it was much cheaper!

CHAPTER SEVENTEEN

During 1988 Ena had regular commitments at the National Film Theatre, half-a-dozen appearances at the Compass Theatre, and several visits to The Plough, Gt. Munden, where she is always well received. On March 11th she gave a lunch-time recital at St. Stephen's Church, Walbrook; a masterpiece by Christopher Wren and, next to St. Paul's, considered to be his finest work. The dome above the centre is an architectural gem, judged to be one of the finest domes in the world, but the 'lump of cheese' sculpture beneath it is less impressive. This was the first of several recitals by Ena at St. Stephens, organised by the, then, organist, Joanna Fraser.

At the end of March, Keith Beckingham, Manager of Chappells of Bond Street, asked Ena to adjudicate in the Yamaha electronic organ competition.

On April 13th, she appeared for the Croydon & Sutton Organ Society at Sutton Civic Centre, and in May with Carl Davis at Leighton House, Kensington. Carl Davis was exhibiting extracts from films to which he had put music, and, much to the delight of the audience, made an impromptu introduction to Ena and they talked about film music.

At the beginning of June, Ena paid a further visit to the Isle of Wight, hosted

'The Umbrella Man' with members of The Compass Theatre, Ickenham, and their official organist (1988).

All stops for lunch! Hill, Norman & Beard Managing Director Frank Fowler and St Stephen Walbrook organist Joana Fraser join Ena at the console prior to her 1989 lunchtime concert at the Church. (photo John D. Sharp).

by Ron Jackson at Luccombe. Ena was met at the (windy) Portsmouth Harbour railway station by Ron's neighbours, Doris and Jim Jolly, who are every bit as nice as they sound, and they conducted her to Ron's house, 'Muffets', at Luccombe. On the Sunday afternoon, Ena gave a concert at Ryde Town Hall on the Walker concert organ, and on the following Wednesday a concert in aid of Cancer Relief, The Earl Mountbatten Hospice and the MacMillan Nurse Appeal, at the Cameo Studio Theatre, Ventnor.

In August there was the annual visit to The Music Museum at Brentford and a concert at Dursley in Gloucestershire. At the end of September, we staged 'This Is My Life' again, this time at the Manor Barn in Bexhill old town, for the Hastings & Bexhill Organ Society. The Manor House at old Bexhill, the oldest parts of which dated from the 13th Century, was restored and enlarged in the 19th Century by the 7th Earl de la Warr (Reginald Sackville), who also enclosed some of the nearby marshland in 1883 by building a sea wall and starting the development that became known as Bexhill-on-Sea. The cattle and fattening shed at the Manor House was transformed into a pavilion, now called the Manor Barn and all that is left of the ancient Manor House. A most atmospheric place in which to perform. Our hosts were Roland and Pamela Acott, who are very kind and enthusiastic and live by the beach at Pevensey Bay.

In October, we staged 'This is My Life' for The Cinema Organ Society at the Fred Tallant Hall near Euston, the first in a series of events designed to celebrate

126

Ena's Sixty Glorious Years in show business, suggested by the then COS London Concert Manager, Victor Patterson. Ena actually made her first public appearance at the age of 14 in 1920, but 1988 was sixty years after she achieved her first solo appointment at a Wurlitzer, at the Tivoli in the Strand.

The celebrations continued on January 18th, when her 83rd birthday was honoured with an evening at the Plough, and on February 1st at the New Gallery, Regent Street, when there was a 'Gala Celebration' and Nigel Ogden introduced John Mann, William Davies, David Lowe and Victor Patterson as guest organists, and when Ena accompanied some silent films.

Towards the end of February, Ena gave a further lunchtime recital at St. Stephen's Walbrook, before a large and appreciative audience. Geoffrey Myers of Croydon recorded the event as follows: 'Did the angels with golden trumpets atop the magnificent organ case of this Wren church in the City of London turn their heads when 'Smoke Gets in Your Eyes' heralded the programme by Ena Baga on Friday, 24th February? They may well have done, as this signature tune was played in authentic Baga style without anyone seated at the console, thanks to the latest device installed on this fine 1888 Hill instrument during its 1987 rebuild by Hill, Norman & Beard. Miss Baga then took her place and treated the enthusiastic audience to a programme of music ranging from Bach to Andrew Lloyd Webber. The occasion was her return visit to St. Stephen as part of the series of Friday lunchtime recitals by theatre, as well as classical, organists that have been a feature of the tenure of the church's own Joanna Fraser.'

'Ena Baga showed her interpretive skill as well as the range and tonal excellence of the organ in all she played, perhaps especially in the Easter Hymn and Intermezzo from Mascagni's 'Cavelleria Rusticana'. Other composers included Bach, Handel, Rossini, Verdi, Tchaikovsky, Wolf-Ferrari, Morton Gould, Richard Rodgers, Andrew Lloyd Webber and Ena Baga herself – represented by her delightful Riverside Reverie; a recollection of a time, she told her audience, when she lived beside the Thames. Frank Fowler, Managing Director of Hill, Norman & Beard, introduced Miss Baga.'

On April 4th we took 'This is My Life' to Eastbourne, and on the 19th Ena played for another silent at the New Gallery, this time for The London & South of England Chapter of the American Theatre Organ Society during their London Safari. Afterwards, Ena took tea with Dr. Edward Mullins from San Francisco at the Meridian Restaurant (former Piccadilly Hotel).

Only five days after a spell in hospital for an eye operation, the gallant Ena was on her travels again, this time with me to Bedworth near Coventry, to present 'This is My Life' to the Bedworth Organ Society. The Working Men's Club at Bedworth lent itself very well to our presentation, and our kind host, as always, was Dorothy ('Poppy') Marcus. Publicity is never far away, and while there Ena made an appearance on Radio West Midlands, interviewed by Chris Giles who played a couple of tracks from her recording at the Odeon Leicester Square; we were both interviewed by the Coventry Evening Telegraph, who devoted hearly half a page to the event plus a very nice photograph.

King's Road, Wimbledon was the venue for a small celebration on August 1st, when Florence reached her 93rd birthday. An old friend of Florence and Ena,

Edith Rawle, came to wish 'Happy Birthday' to Florence, who was looking well and seemed to enjoy the company. Her eyes sparkled when Ena and visiting organist Donald Mackenzie played the little electronic organ in her room.

In October, Ena visited old friends Bob and Pam Heard, who now live in a converted barn at Stinchcombe, near Dursley, Gloucestershire. The former barn is close to their old home, Lamport Court, where, until 1981, they lived with the small Compton pipe organ formerly in the Ritz Cinema at Hereford. Unfortunately, Lamport Court became too big for them and they were forced to sell the beautiful little organ of only four ranks of pipes ('cello, flute, tibia and tromba) and move into their barn, delightfully transformed into a home. There were only three Comptons of four ranks, designed for Union cinemas at Hereford, Horsham and Penzance, the one at Hereford being the best. The 'tromba' was a stop very much favoured by Harold Ramsay Union's Musical Director, and stood in for a trumpet and tuba.

On December 6th, Ena and I were both invited to a launching party at the Odeon Leicester Square for a campaign organised by General Manager Bill Weir and Assistant Manager Malcolm Webb entitled 'Spotlight ODEON-Focus London', due to take place from 6th to 10th December and centred on the Leicester Square Odeon. The theatre opened its doors to the public on three consecutive days, with organised tours of the auditorium, projection box, and etc., and exhibition and a twice-daily slide presentation by myself on the history of the Odeon circuit. The organ was featured for the morning tours by David Lowe, and the whole event culminated on the Sunday with the presentation by the Cinema Organ Society of the Ian Sutherland Award Show, featuring Nigel Ogden at the Compton with the Award-winner for 1989, Martin Harris.

'Woodside' is the name of the home of Mr. and Mrs. Peter Cole at East Cowes on the Isle of Wight. On 23rd April 1990 it was the venue for a concert by Ena on Peter's Wurlitzer pipe organ, which he bought in 1973 shortly after it was ejected from the Ritz Aldershot, where it had been opened by Harold Ramsay in 1937.

Several old friends of Ena's travelled from the mainland for the concert at East Cowes, and there was a capacity audience. The proceeds were donated to the Alexandra Palace Organ Appeal, and over £160 was collected. The newly-opened Isle of Wight Radio took an advertisement in the programme, and the concert was announced on the air in the morning. The console doesn't look so good without its beautiful illuminated surround, but Peter has it safely stored in his garage.

On June 12th Ena was the guest organist at the home of Les and Edith Rawle at Northolt, Wurlitzer Lodge. The concert was before an audience of 56, including Caroline Harris from 'The Independent', who obviously enjoyed herself, as the result was three columns in the paper under a heading 'A sentimental night with the Queen of the Keyboards' and a very nice photograph of Ena at the Rawle residence Wurlitzer console. 'Wurlitzer Lodge is not a normal house', reported Caroline. 'In 1960, its owner Les Rawle bought a cinema organ. Then he bought a plot of land. Then he built a house around the organ and gave it this name, and vowed that every week someone would make the instrument sing. That, briefly, is how the Mighty Wandsworth (sic) Wurlitzer found a home, and why an assorted group of organ buffs have disappeared down the side of a doorless garage every week for the past

30 years . . . It's clear that Miss Ena Baga, at '80-plus', loves life and the accolades she receives from ageing friends and fans . . . At 10.40 Miss Baga was still going strong – doing a rumba. At 10.55 she slid into her theme tune and the mightly Wurlitzer rumbled to a stop. 'We've given it some ammo tonight' she cried. 'Any more for any more?' Miss Baga had outlasted us all.'

The Wurlitzer that Les Rawle bought was in fact that of the Granada Wandsworth Road, opened by Harry Farmer in 1936. He also added pipework from the West End Birmingham and elsewhere, and it is now a powerful instrument. Ena is a frequent performer at Wurlitzer Lodge, the headquarters of the London & South of England Chapter of the American Theatre Organ Society.

On 23rd and 24th June the Compass Theatre appeared at the Middlesex Show at Uxbridge. In their newly-acquired Theatre Big Top, like a small circus tent, they arranged an exhibition and a continuous programme of music hall, melodrama and revue, with Ena Baga at the Yamaha electronic organ.

On the 11th Judy Ena had been a guest on Radio 4's 'Midweek' programme. After the broadcast, Ena sat for a while in Kensington Gardens as it was such a nice early summer day. When she got back to Latymer Court, the porter had a message that Florence had died at 11 o'clock. Florence had been in a very weak condition and hardly conscious when she saw her a day or so previously, so her death was not unexpected. Nevertheless, it is still a shock to those nearest and dearest, and although they had not always seen eye-to-eye and had different characters resulting in frequent arguments, Ena knew that she had not only lost a sister but a lifelong friend.

The obituary in the Daily Telegraph for Florence contained a very nice photograph, taken at the console of the organ at the Gaumont Camden Town. She was cremated at Putney Vale Crematorium on July 16th with a small crowd of friends and admirers including Robin Richmond, John Sherratt from the Compass Theatre, Joe Shaw, Bill and Joan Hiscock, Douglas Badham of the COS, and Lilian and Gina Langsfield, who first met the Baga sisters through an interest in silent films. Florence died just three weeks before her 94th birthday.

'The Show Must Go On', and on the previous day Ena appeared in concert with David Shepherd at the New Gallery. One can only guess what was going through her mind as she sat at the console of the little Model 'F' Wurlitzer that both she and Florence had played together in 1926. On September 4th she was back at the New Gallery, recording a 15-minute interview with Nigel Ogden, together with a little music, for BBC Radio 2's 'The Organist Entertains'.

Matriach in maturity! In her eighties, Florence still enjoyed performing as she did when only a girl of fourteen.

CHAPTER EIGHTEEN

Although Florence had been very much an invalid for the last two or three years of her life, she was still very much 'around' and, even if it meant a journey to Wimbledon and back several times a week, Ena was naturally constantly at Florence's side. Her death was the end of an era in Ena's life and for the first time she felt alone.

On 30th September Ena made one of her visits to Sandford Park, appearing on the Sunday evening with Brian Sharp, resident organist. Two weeks later, she accompanied a Buster Keaton silent at Ashton Manor Golf Club, where the large dining-room and lounge were united to form one auditorium. On November 12th, the new Compass Theatre was opened at Ickenham with the staging of an original intimate revue, 'Imagine', before HRH The Prince Edward. Joining in with the choir and orchestra was Ena at the company's Yamaha, and, before the second half, she played an entr'acte for which she received an ovation. Ena was later presented to Prince Edward and to the Mayor and Mayoress of Ickenham, and had the honour of being appointed official organist to the Compass Theatre. Ena and Florence had been associated with The Compass for twenty years or more, at first to accompany silent films, then at Gala events, on tour and in cabaret. The Compass described Ena as 'an essential part of their package' – on tour in the travelling tent, on their roving truck and in any new venture they were to devise.

To round off 1990, the London chapter of the ATOS presented Ena in concert with American singing organist, Lowell Ayars, in a special Christmas show at the Top Rank Club, Kilburn.

1991 began in style for Ena with a special performance at the National Film Theatre on January 10th. As a tribute to Florence the NFT screened one of her favourite films, 'The Thief of Bagdad'. Starring, and directed by, Douglas Fairbanks, the film was made in the USA and is 135 minutes long, Ena providing the entire accompaniment at the grand piano. After $2\frac{1}{4}$ hours of sympathetic music (including Borodin and excerpts from the overture 'The Caliph of Bagdad'), the lady was a little fatigued but was greatly revived with red wine thoughtfully provided by the management. Manager, Leslie Hardcastle, and Assistant Vanda Jones joined us, together with invited guests, including Hill, Norman & Beard M.D. Frank Fowler and Edith and Les Rawle of the ATOS.

January 15th was Ena's 85th birthday, and Frank Fowler arranged a surprise dinner-party at an Italian restaurant in Friern Barnet. Ena thought she was having a quiet evening on her own with Frank; imagine her surprise when I popped out of the kitchen and when we were later joined by Richard Cole and Owen Cooper from The Music Museum and Dennis Wells, Frank's travelling organ technician! Our one regret was that the erstwhile organist of St. Stephen Walbrook, Joanna Fraser, was not well enough to join us.

Three days later, Ena appeared in concert with one of the other great names from the heyday of the theatre organ, Louis Mordish, at the Cinema Organ Society's

Mighty classical man meets Mighty Wurlitzer lady! Ena chats with Carlo Curley at the Worthing tribute to Bobby Pagan in 1991. (photo: John D. Sharp).

Mighty Wurlitzer at the South Bank Polytechnic. Louis Mordish also began his career as a pianist in silent days; but became an orchestral pianist, joining Joseph Muscant at the Commodore Hammersmith and moving with him to the Troxy Stepney. In 1936, he successfully auditioned as theatre organist with the Hyams Brothers, who owned the Troxy and the Trocadero Elephant & Castle among other theatres, playing at the Regal West Norwood and Gaumont Watford until call-up to the RAF in 1941. Demob in 1946 saw his appointment to the New Victoria cinema in London, and from 1947 he toured Gaumont-British theatres, based at the Gaumont Camden Town, Gaumont Chelsea and Trocadero Elephant & Castle. From 1952 to 1953 he was at the Gaumont State Kilburn, and his last theatre organ residency was from 1953 to 1958 at the Leicester Square Theatre.

Since 1958, Louis has free-lanced, as M.D. for summer seasons; playing film preludes at the Odeon Swiss Cottage; M.D. for 'Annie' at the Westminster Theatre; and for many years touring the world as Musical Director to Dickie Henderson. He has been a regular broadcaster for nearly 60 years and is a most prolific composer, often appearing as conductor of his own symphonic suite 'A Legend of the Woods'. Louis has a great reputation for interpretation of light classics at which he is an undoubted master, but he does not neglect the popular tune!

A week after her appearance at the South Bank with Louis, Ena was at the Fairfield Hall Croydon, doing something she first did some 65 years before at the Strand Cinema Southend – playing for silents.

One of the organists with whom Louis Mordish had a close association was

Bobby Pagan, and together they toured the Gaumont-British circuit just after the Second World War playing piano and organ duets. On May 26th, Louis and Ena joined forces with Douglas Reeve, Robin Richmond and Bobby Pagan's pupil, Michael Wooldridge, to pay a special tribute to Bobby (who died in the previous December) at the Worthing Wurlitzer. Ena topped the first half of the bill, including a lovely version of that beautiful melody written for the film of the same name, 'Laura'; at the grand piano, Louis played the first and last pieces that he and Bobby had performed together at GB theatres – 'Dizzy Fingers' and Brahms' 'Hungarian Dance No. 6', returning to the console of the Wurlitzer for an impeccable and exhilarating version of 'The Caliph of Bagdad'.

On June 8th Frank Fowler was Ena's guest at the Annual Dinner of the Cinema & Television Benevolent Fund at the Royal Lancaster Hotel. At the end of the month, Ena paid a return visit to the Malvern Cinema Organ Club, where there was almost a full house. She was driven there by neighbours Eric and Stella Peet, and they stayed at the Peet's house at Little Aston, about ten miles from Lichfield in Staffordshire.

'Keyboard Queen visits Shanklin' said the Isle of Wight County Press on July 5th, the day before Ena gave a recital in aid of Guide Dogs for the Blind at St. Saviour's-on-the-Cliff church, Shanklin. Chairman of the Island Guide Dogs charity, Derek Oxlade, was quoted: 'Events like this are a great help to us on the Island. We do not have many huge businesses sponsoring us like mainland branches do. Miss Baga organised virtually everything. The concert was splendid, and we will use the money to support the 16 guide dogs we have on the Island.' The organ, an old Walker, was not in too good condition, Ena told us, but the concert went well and the press reported a total of £300 raised. Ena was also interviewed on the radio.

Ena has always thought that Florence and herself were the last of the family line. Sister Celeste lost her little girl with meningitis; Florence lost Pauline through a road accident; and Beatrice's son, Harold, died prematurely. However, out of the blue, Ena received a letter from a relative in the USA. As children Ena and Florence took regular holidays at Herne Bay in Kent with their Uncle Nathaniel, or 'Uncle Nat' as they always called him. Uncle Nat, Constantine Baga's brother, and Auntie Annie had one son, Ben, who was first violin and leader of the Folkestone Municipal Orchestra. Ben's first marriage was to Pauline Olga Hill, and they had two children, Kathy and Pauline. By his second marriage, Ben had a son, David, and it was David's daughter, Julie Adriana Baga who wrote to Ena from the USA, where she is a librarian and her sister, Susan, is a violinist (music in the blood!).

In September, 1991, Julie came to stay with Ena at Latymer Court for a week, and a kind friend of Ena's, Maggie Southgate, hosted a party at her house in Turnham Green so that we could meet. Friends Jane Ryan and Yvonne Smith made up the party. It was a most enjoyable and memorable evening, all too short, and Julie Baga showed that she had inherited the Baga personality and intelligence.

In October, publishers Stainer & Bell had a bit of a 'ding-dong', if they will parden the pun. It was actually a house-warming to celebrate their move to Victoria House, Finchley, during which they staged a ceremony to inaugurate their

Compton Melotone electronic organ. Compton invented the 'Melotone' (at first called Melophone) in 1934/35, and at first it was an electronic unit attached to most of their theatre organ installations from 1935 to 1939. At the equivalent of 8 feet, 4 feet and 2 feet pitches, this device produced the most beautiful mellow tones (hence the name), and when these were combined with the flute, say, or the tibia (stopped flute), the effect was outstanding. Variations on the standard tone were available, e.g. a nasal variety called krummhorn and a cor anglais. The unit also produced chimes and vibraphone, and some even had a glide effect to imitate the Hawaiian guitar! Later, the system was developed into a complete electronic organ, the 'Theatrone' (the church model was the 'Electrone'), the post-war version of which was the Compton Melotone.

The one purchased by Stainer & Bell is believed to have been installed in an Isle of Wight cinema, and a subsequent owner had built an illuminated surround for it complete with colour-change, and had disguised it to look like a cinema organ console. The organ was opened at Finchley by Nigel Ogden, who also cut a cake baked in the shape of the instrument. Ena was one of the guests and she gave a short interlude, followed by duets by Nigel and Louis Mordish at the piano. Ena's composition, 'Bagatelle', which she used as a signature tune for a while instead of 'Smoke Gets in Your Eyes', was shortly to be published by Stainer & Bell, who had already published several compositions by Nigel Ogden.

At the end of November, Ena was invited to Holland, to accompany some Buster Keaton silents at the Passage Theatre Schiedam. The arrangements for our visit were made by Jack Raves, and everything went very smoothly. Jack and Ria Raves met us for dinner on the Saturday night, and, in spite of the fog, took us on a tour of Utrecht, ancient and modern. I was pleased to catch a glimpse of one or two of the super trams! We stayed overnight at Vianen, close to the Lek river, and next day taken to Schiedam, near Rotterdam, for the afternoon film show, consisting of three Keaton comedies and one of Keaton in a most serious role, simply entitled 'Film'. Ena received a standing ovation, a huge bouquet of flowers and a reception fit for a queen! The Dutch really are a most hospitable people, and we could not have been better looked after! They certainly like their silent films, and a more organ-minded country could not exist. Not only for the famous Dutch street-organs, but they had their own manufacturers of theatre organs, e.g. Standaart, some of which were imported to the UK. Strangely, they had few theatre organists of note, the most famous being Cor Steyn who years after his death is still revered by young and old alike. One of the officials we met was named Reginald – after Reginald Dixon!

1992 began with Charles Chaplin, or rather a film about him. On 23rd January, Ena was taken to Shepperton Studios to play to a slapstick comedy in a mock-up of a funeral parlour converted into an early picture palace. Dressed in a long black frock and a wig, she doubted if anyone would recognise her! The film, called 'Chaplin' and directed by Sir Richard Attenborough was released during 1992, and had its charity premiere at the Odeon Leicester Square, with Ena at the organ and a personal appearance by Sir Richard.

On February 10th, Ena was the special guest for an evening with the Cinema Organ Society in London, in a presentation on the lines of the BBC Radio 4

'I first played here 66 years ago'. Ena at the 1992 'Farewell to the New Gallery Wurlitzer', presented by the COS. (photo: John D. Sharp).

programme, 'Desert Island Discs', but with the title 'Desert Island Organ Discs'. The evening went very well, Ena choosing, among others, Quentin Maclean's 'Happy Days selection', to remind her of the Strand Cinema Southend; Florence at the New Gallery playing her signature tune 'Passing Thoughts', composed for her by their father; Jessie Matthews singing 'Everything's In Rhythm With My Heart', to remind her of the visit to the Regent Sheffield; Louis Levy & The Gaumont British Symphony playing the GB News theme ('Music From The Movies') and a song from the Fred Astaire film 'Shall We Dance', a film shown at the Gaumont Camden Town while she was there; Harry Roy and His Band to remind her of her first Sunday concert at Blackpool Tower, which she shared with Anne Ziegler and Webster Booth, and Harry Roy's Ragamuffins; one of her own recordings at the Tower of wartime songs, including the memorable version of 'Yes, My Darling Daughter'; Bill Davies playing Mendelssohn's 'Scherzo to Midsummer Night's Dream', to remind her of Tottenham Court Road; Joseph Seal playing Toselli's 'Serenata', which was Sir Roy Welensky's favourite; George Wright playing Harry Warren songs at the Paramount Oakland; and a medley of songs from Amsterdam played by Cor Steyn. In short, a potted version of Ena's life, before a very enthusiastic audience.

After more than 65 years, the little Model 'F' Wurlitzer at the New Gallery so loved by Florence during her thirteen years residency, looked likely to go during 1992. The Seventh Day Adventist Church acquired the lease in the 1950s for a Church Centre but, although the drums, cymbals and other effects were removed, the Wurlitzer otherwise remained as installed in 1925, the first in the West End – and the last! The Cinema Organ Society, which had been looking after the Wurlitzer, staged a 'Farwell to the New Gallery' on March 22nd to mark the sad removal of the organ, which, with the departure of the Seventh Day Adventists, seemed inevitable. Ena accompanied silent classics of the twenties, as she first did there in 1926, and the COS Deputy Chairman, David Lowe, featured the organ in concert.

And so, at the grand age of 87, Ena continues the Baga tradition of entertaining the public, just as her father and three sisters have done for the best part of the Twentieth Century. She has yet to appear on ITV's 'This Is Your Life' and BBC Radio 4's 'Desert Island Discs', but she would be an excellent subject for both and we live in hopes. 1992 has seen the publication of her 'Bagatelle', a catchy number that for some years she used as a signature tune. We hope that this book will prove to be an entertaining and informative account of events in the life of Ena and her family.

INDEX